DOW 40,000

DOW 40,000
Strategies for Profiting from the Greatest Bull Market in History

DAVID ELIAS

McGraw-Hill

New York San Francisco Washington, D.C. Auckland Bogotá
Caracas Lisbon London Madrid Mexico City Milan
Montreal New Delhi San Juan Singapore
Sydney Tokyo Toronto

Library of Congress Cataloging-in-Publication Data

Elias, David.
   Dow 40,000 : strategies for profiting from the greatest bull
market in history / by David Elias.
     p.   cm.
   ISBN 0-07-135128-0
   1. Investments—United States. 2. Stock exchanges—United States.
3. Dow Jones industrial average. I. Title. II. Title: Dow forty
thousand.
   HG4910.E45 1999
   332.63'22—dc21
                                    99-28747
                                    CIP

McGraw-Hill

*A Division of The **McGraw·Hill** Companies*

1 2 3 4 5 6 7 8 9 0   DOC/DOC   9 0 9 8 7 6 5 4 3 2 1 0 9

ISBN 0-07-135128-0

This publication is designed to provide accurate and authoritative information in regard to the subject matter covered. It is sold with the understanding that neither the author nor the publisher is engaged in rendering legal, accounting, futures/securities trading, or other professional service. If legal advice or other expert assistance is required, the services of a competent professional person should be sought.
        —*From a Declaration of Principles jointly adopted by a Committee of the American Bar Association and a Committee of Publishers.*

The sponsoring editor for this book was Kelli Christiansen, the editing supervisor was Barry Brown, and the production supervisor was Elizabeth Strange. It was set in Melior by Jana Fisher through the services of Barry E. Brown (Broker—Editing, Design and Production).

Printed and bound by R.R. Donnelley & Sons Company.

McGraw-Hill books are available at special quantity discounts to use as premiums and sales promotions, or for use in corporate training programs. For more information, please write to the Director of Special Sales, McGraw-Hill, 11 West 19th Street, New York, NY 10011. Or contact your local bookstore.

This book is printed on recycled, acid-free paper containing a minimum of 50% recycled, de-inked fiber.

CONTENTS

Chapter 3

Social Security, Economics 101, and a Booming Economy   47

Chapter 4

Demographics and the "Post-Capitalist Society"   71

Chapter 5

Interest Rates and Inflation   79

Chapter 9

Chapter 10

FOREWORD

Many professionals on Wall Street today have experienced only the good times. In the market for less than a decade, they often cannot distinguish between a true long-term Bull Market and so-called "irrational exuberance."

David Elias can.

When I first heard David talk about a Dow 40,000, I knew that his prediction must be based on solid research. Over the many years that I have known David Elias, I have been continually impressed by his clear thinking, prudent approach, and first-hand experience.

His enthusiasm about the wealth-creating potential of investing is grounded in a profound understanding of the economic landscape. He has tracked the new renaissance of capitalism here and around the world and the achievements of the technological revolution. David's optimism is based on the exciting future this portends, and he shares some successful strategies for thriving in the Age of the Investor.

As one of the oldest established Wall Street firms—founded in 1924—Trainer, Wortham is proud to be serving a national base that includes fourth-generation clients. Today's investors are far more involved in charting their financial futures than were their counterparts years ago. They highly value practical and understandable financial information.

Dow 40,000 is exactly that. It is an excellent book for individual investors. The author explains the fundamentals and provides common-sense guidance to investing for the long term. Here is a beacon to help investors stay the course during times of change and volatility.

This book is a fine companion to take along on the journey to Dow 40,000.

Charles V. Moore, President
Trainer, Wortham & Company, Inc.

INTRODUCTION

The idea to write a book about the stock market and its potential to create wealth evolved from the many conversations I had with Elias Asset Management clients for more than two decades. My first foray into writing a full-length book came in 1998. It was composed of six chapters, tracing the history of the Dow Jones Industrial Average, providing a snapshot of economic conditions in 1997, and pinpointing noteworthy trends. All of that material was revised for this book. However, *Dow 40,000* is much more than an update. Four new chapters have been included, covering basic investor information.

Dow 40,000 may be two books in one. Readers with a strong interest in the history of the stock market and the economic fundamentals underlying it are likely to be attracted to the first six chapters. Here they will be introduced to classical, as well as contemporary economic concepts, definitions of terms, global economic and market perspectives, the dynamics of interest rates and inflation, and social policy. And it is these first six chapters that build the case for my conviction that the Dow Jones Industrial Average will reach 40,000 by 2016.

Those of you seeking investment themes and opportunities to march to Dow 40,000 will be especially interested in the final four chapters. Here you will find the winning investment strategies that I have identified for the next 20 years. You can also learn about common stocks, mutual funds, and innovative products that Wall Street has developed to simplify investing. Further, I have designed a series of model portfolios in Chapter 10.

Today we understand that the only constant is change. Whether in medicine or technology, on Capitol Hill or in foreign capitals, on Earth or in space, we cannot begin to fathom all the changes ahead. The wise lessons of history teach us not to fear change, but to embrace its endless possibilities.

As the world around us changes, I am certain that the stock market will not move in an unchanging straight line to achieve Dow 40,000. There will be normal fluctuations and market pullbacks. However, I am convinced that the overall movement will continue in the right direction: up. The first and second sections of this book pave the road to Dow

40,000, where you'll learn why I am optimistic about the stock market for at least 20 years into the twenty-first century.

Having a long-term investment strategy is the road that has proved successful over the years. I believe the reliable road will lead to Dow 40,000. Consequently, I will donate all profits from the sale of *Dow 40,000* to schools and other organizations dedicated to advancing the education and well-being of America's greatest resource: young people.

David Elias

ACKNOWLEDGMENTS

According to an ancient maxim, when the student is ready, the teacher will appear. Certain individuals have come into my life, and I have learned from each of them. I deeply value their contributions over the years, and acknowledge their parts directly or indirectly in making this book a reality.

When I was growing up in Geneva, New York, I knew two extraordinary teachers, Gil Epley and William R. Grammar. In college, I was encouraged by Howard E. Kiefer, Ph.D. I am grateful for the advice on the craft of writing from my friend Lee Coppola, dean of the Russell J. Jandoli School of Journalism and Mass Communication at St. Bonaventure University.

Jack and Kay Connell, Nolan Johannes, Fred Mackerodt, Bill Townsend, and Frank Zachary, all of whom believed in me and provided important early opportunities, have become mentors and friends, as was the late Msgr. John G. Clancy.

Ken Sarpu first suggested that I write this book. Terri Brunsdon presented the concept to McGraw-Hill, where I have had the good fortune to work with the expert team of Jeffrey Krames and Kelli Christiansen. They believe, as I do, that providing useful financial information to readers is a worthwhile endeavor.

Mary Ann Lauricella has been a close friend for 25 years. Having her as project manager of *Dow 40,000* gave me the confidence that we could achieve our goals and meet our deadlines.

Nick Verbanic ably led the research effort, assisted by Jeff Suchocki, Kristin Linthwaite, John Shine, and Tom Metzler. I am grateful for the superb editing skills of Pat Donlon and for the graphic design work of Chet Kozlowski.

The counsel of Peter Greco, a close friend since the 1970s and who shares my passion for the stock market, was invaluable, as was the support of my administrative assistant, Mari Ann Galus.

My wife, Barbara, a loving family, talented associates, and loyal clients and friends helped make this book possible. For that, I am forever grateful.

PART ONE

SETTING THE STAGE FOR A SOARING DOW

CHAPTER 1

By the Numbers

The first six chapters in Part 1 contain basic reference material that can help you understand the myriad factors—historical and contemporary—that shape the market environment. The facts, figures, charts, and graphs might find a useful place in your personal library.

Despite the increasing attention that the popular media focus on the stock market in the daily news, the general public seems confused about exactly what the "market" is. More specifically, what is the Dow Jones Industrial Average (DJIA)? Some of the more elementary questions about the DJIA, or the "Dow," are addressed in this chapter. Facts and figures that support our position that the DJIA will reach 40,000 by 2016 are included, as well as the opinions of some of the world's top economists.

HISTORY

The Dow Jones Industrial Average was created by Charles Dow, one of the founders of Dow Jones and Company. Along with co-founder Edward Jones, Dow produced the first reputable information source for businesses with the creation of the *Customer's Afternoon Letter.* Near the end of the nineteenth century, stock investment was highly speculative. Stock values were wildly affected by rumors, often created by corrupt business executives who stood to profit by the spread of false information. Reliable information was at a premium and nearly impossible to come by.

Dow very quickly developed a reputation as an honest and upstanding individual, winning the favor of many of the era's top business leaders. He was trusted to provide accurate information involving the business dealings of the day. Eventually, his reputation led to a boom in business and to the founding of *The Wall Street Journal* on July 8, 1889.

In May 1896, the Dow Jones Industrial Average made its debut. The original index contained 12 stocks, of which General Electric Company is the only remaining member (GE was dropped in 1898 but was later added to replace Tennessee Coal & Iron). The index was increased to 20 stocks in 1916 and then to 30 in 1928, where it remains today.

The criteria for selecting member stocks have remained remarkably consistent over the years. The index is generally composed of large firms that have established themselves over time as market and industry leaders.

See Table 1-1. In the history of the DJIA, there have been only 45 company changes, 24 of them during the Great Depression.

Since 1940, there have been only 21 changes, most of which were made because of notable corporate actions such as divestitures, mergers, or bankruptcies. Whenever there is a change in one of the companies, all of the companies are then reviewed for their suitability. Obviously, continuity is one of the Dow's strengths.

Over the years, the DJIA has done a remarkable job of mirroring the changes of U.S. industry, following the shift from an agricultural-based through an industrial-based to today's technology-based economy. The index originally contained commodities companies, electric and gas utilities, and streetcar and railroad firms. As other industries gained in importance, so did their representation in the index.

The first third of the century saw the addition of several automobile companies, as passenger cars gained significance in American life. The additions of Hewlett-Packard, Johnson & Johnson, Citigroup, and Wal-Mart have followed the shift from a manufacturing economy to a service- and technology-based economy. What I see happening over the next 20 years are more changes in the index composition, representing new technology. Companies such as Intel Corporation, Lucent Technologies, Microsoft Corporation, and America Online Inc. may be represented.

IS THE DOW A GOOD YARDSTICK?

Now more than a century old, the DJIA has become the symbol of American economic health. It's little wonder, considering that the 30 stocks represented in the Dow account for approximately one-fifth of the total market

TABLE 1-1

The DJIA Then and Now

Original 12 stocks in the DJIA

American Sugar	National Lead
American Tobacco	North American
Chicago Gas	Tennessee Coal & Iron
Distilling & Cattle Feeding	U.S. Leather preferred
General Electric Company	U.S. Rubber
Laclede Gas	American Cotton Oil

Current 30 stocks in the DJIA

AT&T Corp.	Goodyear Tire & Rubber Company
Alcoa Inc.	Hewlett-Packard
AlliedSignal Inc.	International Business Machines Corp.
American Express Company	International Paper Company
Boeing Co.	Johnson & Johnson
Caterpillar Inc.	McDonald's Corporation
Chevron Corporation	Merck & Co., Inc.
Citigroup Inc.	Minnesota Mining and Manufacturing Corp.
Coca-Cola Company	J.P. Morgan & Co., Incorporated
Walt Disney Company	Philip Morris Companies Inc.
E. I. Du Pont de Nemours and Company	Procter & Gamble Company
Eastman Kodak Co.	Sears, Roebuck & Co.
Exxon Corporation	Union Carbide Corporation
General Electric Company	United Technologies Corporation
General Motors Corporation	Wal-Mart Stores, Inc.

value of the $11.3 trillion U. S. equity market. But is this an accurate application of the Dow? How well does the Dow correlate with the economy?

Many market analysts believe that the general public's perception of the Dow as an economic indicator is an inaccurate assessment of how things actually are. Perhaps because of its grand history and great visibility, Americans have become conditioned to associate the market with the Dow. Market followers have often noted that the Dow provides a strong indication of economic activity in the ensuing one to two years. There are, of course, many different ways to define the market.

Some people take the Dow too seriously. They think it will flawlessly predict the future. In fact, some analysts have humorously reported that the market has predicted nine of the last five recessions. While the experts debate the validity of the Dow as a forecasting tool, there is no argument that the general direction of the Dow certainly affects the public's perception of the state of the economy and where it is headed in the near future. And since two-thirds of the United States' Gross Domestic Product (GDP) is derived from consumer demand, the public's perception of the economy does seem to be as important as reality.

Regardless of its shortcomings, the DJIA represents a solid historical measure of market performance. For a snapshot of present economic and market conditions, it probably is the best measure.

The Dow's success is as much a cultural phenomenon as anything else. Just about everyone understands what it represents. The Dow took 76 years from its inception to reach the 1,000 mark in 1972. Fifteen years later, in 1987, it marked 2,000. In 1991, the Dow topped 3,000, and four years later, it achieved 4,000. Since 1995, the Dow has taken less than 12 months for each new 1,000-point milestone—crossing 10,000 in March 1999.

The Dow stood largely unchallenged as *the* market index until 1928, when Standard & Poor's Corporation created the S&P 90. The 500 Composite Stock Price Index, or S&P 500, derived from the original S&P 90, debuted on March 4, 1957. The S&P 500 differs from the DJIA in that it is a market capitalization-weighted index. That is, for a given percentage change in the value of a stock, the firm with the larger total market value of its equity will have a greater effect on the index. This is in contrast to the DJIA, which is a price-weighted index.

The S&P 500 number is calculated by computing the total market value of the 500 firms in the index versus the total market value of those firms on the prior day of trading. The percentage change in the total market value from a starting date to an ending date represents the change in the index.

In fact, the DJIA is really not an average at all. Since 1928, the care-takers of the Dow have used a special divisor, instead of simply the number of stocks. The divisor has gone through multiple changes, because of stock splits or changes in companies constituting the index. Those changes have moved the divisor closer to zero, which has increased the volatility of the Dow. The year 1999 began with a divisor of 0.2428, which meant that a one-point gain in a Dow stock added 4.12 points to the average. Investors can calm themselves when the Dow is down 120 points by saying, "Oh, well, each Dow stock is down only a dollar."

Critics say that the DJIA is a crude market measure. I don't believe so. The industrial average is useful for several reasons. As a barometer of blue chip companies, the cream of American industry, it tracks the market with broader, more sophisticated indexes. Furthermore, it is the only index with more than a century of market history and lore. Further, to Americans, the Dow is firmly ingrained in their psyches as "The Market." I might have titled this book S&P 5500 (approximately equivalent to Dow 40,000), but most individual investors would not have been able to relate at all to that number.

40,000 BY 2016?

Based on my own 25 years of experience investing in the stock market, I have developed profound respect for the American economy. The trends that I foresee for the stock market over the next two decades convince me that the DJIA will reach 40,000 by 2016. The reaction I get from clients and investors when I project the Dow to reach 40,000 invariably is skepticism. Even with the Dow averages at unprecedented levels, investors are skeptical of seemingly outlandish predictions, and rightly so. To them, Dow 40,000 is still very much a dream.

It will take time, patience, and wise money management by investors, corporations, and government entities before the economy and the market can support price levels of that nature. I have projected 2016 as the target date for the Dow to break 40,000.

When he was teaching finance at the Columbia University Graduate School of Business, Benjamin Graham had never awarded an A+ until a special student entered his class. The student was eager to begin his investment career, but the professor advised otherwise. The year was 1951, and the Dow had yet to fall below its previous-year high, something it had done every year since its inception. The professor advised his A+ student to wait until after the Dow dropped below 200, and then to begin investing. The student ignored his mentor's advice and invested around

$10,000. Today, Warren Buffett has seen his initial $10,000 investment grow into a fortune of billions and is considered by many to be the best investor in history.

In other words, whenever the market reaches a new high, or a level that seems too high, veteran investors become cautious. They have learned from experience to be wary of an exuberant market, a psychological dynamic, which inevitably breaks when enough time passes. More important, this story illustrates the danger of missing a bull market. If Buffett had taken his teacher's advice, he'd probably still have the original $10,000. It's been said before: more money has been lost in preparing for a bear market than in the bear market itself.

Buffett's tremendous success illustrates another important concept: that of compound interest. Albert Einstein referred to compound interest as "the most powerful force in the universe." An example of what can happen when an individual waits for the Dow to indicate "the perfect time" to invest is the saga of Joe, a friend of mine. Joe started calling me in 1982 when the Dow was just over 1,000, looking for the right time to get into equities. Over the years, he continued to seek a pullback that would be his perfect moment. Today, at age 62, Joe still has his money parked in bank CDs. He has missed the entire bull market and all its thousand-point milestones. Even now, Joe does not realize that there never is a perfect time. When the market recovers from a pullback, it generally goes to new highs.

To illustrate the power of compound interest, consider "the Dutch who bought Manhattan Island from the Indians for about $24. If the Indians had placed the money in a compound interest account, their heirs could afford to buy back the island today, including the Empire State Building, World Trade Center, and all the 'improvements' since the seventeenth century."[1]

Or consider that a $100 investment in the Dow in 1900 would have grown into a fortune in excess of $70 million as of year-end 1998. That is an impressive demonstration not only of the wealth-generating power of blue chip equities, but also of the power of compounding over long periods.

We have already discussed the power of compound rates and how they affect the DJIA. Another illustration may be effective in illuminating its awesome force. Figure 1-1 shows how different compounding interest rates affect terminal wealth after 20 years, from an initial investment of $10,000.

---

[1]Buchholz, Todd G. 1980. *New Ideas from Dead Economists.* New York: Penguin Books, p. 47.

FIGURE 1-1

Investing for the Long Term Creates Wealth

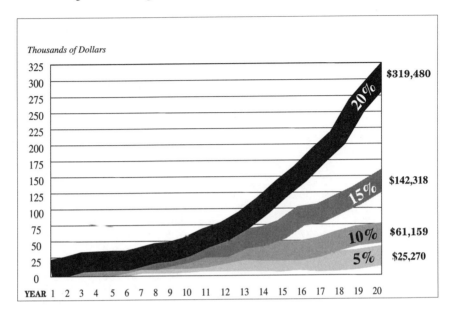

THE KEY IS LONG-TERM GROWTH

Exactly how much annual growth is actually necessary to reach 40,000 by 2016? A compound-interest analysis shows that annual growth of just 9 percent projects the Dow to reach 40,000 some time in 2016, as shown in Table 1-2. More aggressive annual growth rates of 11 or 12 percent project the Dow reaching 40,000 in 2012 and 2011, respectively.

Although I am taking the conservative approach and projecting that the Dow will reach 40,000 by 2016, it would not surprise me to see it reach 40,000 before then. In fact, between December 31, 1982, and December 31, 1998, a portfolio invested in the Dow 30 would have returned an investor an average annual return of 18.4 percent.

Economist Lawrence Kudlow of American Skandia Life Assurance Inc. says, "From 1982 to 1995, the Dow Jones Industrial Average increased 300 percent (adjusted for inflation), or 11 percent per year . . . Along the way, roughly 100 million Americans who own stocks and bonds . . . saw their net worth go up by an extraordinary $10 trillion, a 176 percent gain, which annualizes to 8.1 percent. From this rising wealth

TABLE 1-2

The Dow's Run to 40,000					
Year End	8%	9%	10%	11%	12%
1998	9,000	9,000	9,000	9,000	9,000
1999	9,720	9,810	9,900	9,990	10,080
2000	10,498	10,693	10,890	11,089	11,290
2001	11,337	11,655	11,979	12,309	12,644
2002	12,244	12,704	13,177	13,663	14,162
2003	13,224	13,848	14,495	15,166	15,861
2004	14,282	15,094	15,944	16,834	17,764
2005	15,424	16,452	17,538	18,685	19,896
2006	16,658	17,933	19,292	20,741	22,284
2007	17,991	19,547	21,222	23,022	24,958
2008	19,430	21,306	23,344	25,555	27,953
2009	20,985	23,224	25,678	28,366	31,307
2010	22,664	25,314	28,246	31,486	35,064
2011	24,477	27,592	31,070	34,950	39,271
2012	26,435	30,076	34,177	38,794	43,984
2013	28,550	32,782	37,595	43,061	49,262
2014	30,833	35,733	41,355	47,798	55,174
2015	33,300	38,949	45,490	53,056	61,794
2016	35,964	42,454	50,039	58,892	69,210
2017	38,841	46,275	55,043	65,370	77,515
2018	41,949	50,440	60,547	72,561	86,817
2010	45,305	54,979	66,602	80,542	97,235
2020	48,929	59,927	73,262	89,402	108,903
2021	52,843	65,321	80,589	99,236	121,971

base, the U.S. economy created 29 million new jobs and produced a whopping 43 percent gain in real disposable income."[2]

Kudlow believes Americans are better off because the measures fail to take into account benefits such as health care, retirement programs, vacations, holidays, and sick leave which represent, in effect, an increase in income. I will discuss other reasons for my rational exuberance throughout the book, but first, what is it going to take to get there? What has to happen to create the proper environment for the economy to flourish and grow as it was meant to?

---

[2]Kudlow, Lawrence. 1996. "Crossroads," *National Review,* 20 May, p. 36.

HOW DO WE GET THERE?

Historically, the annual return on the stock market in the United States is approximately 10 percent, although it has been rising. As Table 1-2 shows, higher growth rates present an incredible opportunity for wealth creation. I believe that there is no single event that will thrust the DJIA to 40,000. Rather, a combination of several dynamic forces working in unison will fuel the economy to drive the Dow to new heights.

I have identified several trends that support my confidence and will drive a new and vigorous market. Those forces include foreign ownership of U.S. financial assets, the current and future domestic savings binge, the movement toward a balanced federal budget, low to no inflation, declining interest rates, and a cooperative central bank policy. Accelerated advances in technology, including greater use of the Internet for all phases of economic activity, will be a significant factor. These variables are a direct result, as well as a cause, of the so-called "New Economy." Combined with some of the present investment trends, the ideal environment for robust growth appears to be in place. Before we look at these trends, let's first brush up on economics.

THE NEW ECONOMY

The media and investors have focused much attention on the New Economy and its implications for the stock market. Most applied economic models today suggest that as economic growth accelerates and the gap between actual GDP and potential GDP narrows, inflation will occur. Soon after, interest rates will rise, economic growth will slow, and the economy will enter a recession. However, in the late twentieth-century expansion, this typical business cycle did not manifest itself. Economic growth was steady, interest rates remained low, and inflation was benign. The New Economy theory explains this apparent paradox.

The concept of the New Economy is based on the fact that the economic environment of the 1990s was unlike any seen before. The Cold War was over, and the world was at relative peace, thus enabling resources to flow freely from government military projects to consumer projects. Nations opened their markets to foreign competition. Further, the information superhighway created an entirely new facet of the economy, frequently called the cyber economy. In this environment, physical borders do not exist. Price competition is the rule, and currency differentials can be resolved quickly and efficiently. The launching of the euro in 1999 as the single currency for 11 European nations was a signal event. At the outset, commercial transactions were settled in cyberspace: among computers, not with the transfer of hard currency and coins.

Today, competition truly takes place at a global level. This trend is forcing business to adopt new disciplines to remain competitive. Business must attain optimal efficiency to survive. This forced productivity expands the rate at which the economy can grow, as systems and people become increasingly productive.

As long as the political leaders of the world behave themselves, there is little reason to believe that this environment will not continue. As a result, low interest rates, low inflation, and high economic growth can indeed coexist. The economic models of the recent past, which suggest that the market has extended the good times beyond their normal life span, may need to be re-evaluated.

DIRECT FOREIGN INVESTMENT

Direct foreign investment (DFI) is when a company anywhere in the world makes an investment in a foreign company's hard assets, such as plant and equipment. The investment can be an outright purchase of the company, infusion of capital, or a transfer of technology. The desired result is establishing a controlling interest in that business and bolstering the investing company's impact on the foreign country's economy. In 1998, DFI in the United States was $101 billion. In addition to DFI, European investors alone bought more than $70 billion in U.S. equities.

I don't believe that foreign investments in U.S. assets present any problems for Corporate America. Foreign investors have built factories in this country, about the highest caliber vote of confidence that can be made in the U.S. economy. These brick and mortar investments by DFI are perhaps most evident in the automobile industry. Mercedes-Benz, BMW, Nissan, and Toyota all have established plants within the United States, reflecting a process called "instant manufacturing." This is when firms move their operations closer to the customer, allowing businesses to take advantage of cost efficiencies while remaining flexible to customer demands.

Given the influence of international factors, there is concern over the appreciating U.S. dollar and the possibly negative impact it will have on American equities. The dollar traditionally has been a flight-to-quality financial asset for the international community, especially in times of political unrest. However, despite relative peace in the world, the dollar remains in strong demand in foreign markets. This is in spite of a rising merchandise trade deficit.

So, what accounts for the advancing dollar in light of the trade deficit? One explanation is the vast interest rate differentials between the United States and foreign markets, especially in Japan, where interest rates have remained in the 1–2 percent range. The capital inflows have simply created a demand for the dollar, which has outweighed the influence of the trade deficit, leading to the appreciation. Another explanation is the generally affirmative view held by foreigners of the U.S. economy.

The fundamentals of the American economy are far superior to those of other countries, which is recognized by foreign investors. As the models of the classical economists would predict, foreign investors adjust their portfolios appropriately in order to maximize their returns. In this case, American assets are earning a superior risk-adjusted rate of return compared with other available assets. And because the dollar has maintained or even increased in value compared to the operative foreign currency, the cycle has continued. Foreign capital is important because it helps alleviate pressures placed on U.S. interest rates by excessive public and private borrowing.

Some economists advance a more intriguing argument, that the trade deficit does not capture the underlying fundamental changes in the way that American business conducts overseas trade. Production is becoming more mobile because companies are becoming more global. United States companies have long-standing investments in other countries. That accounts for a portion of the U.S. trade deficit.

For example, when General Electric manufactures lightbulbs in Hungary and ships them to the United States, they are considered imports, counting as part of the trade deficit. Other countries, likewise, have been making investments in the United States. When American-made products are shipped to the home country, they count as U.S. exports.

I believe that DFI will increase in the United States as foreign firms seek to take advantage of decreased transaction costs and a highly skilled domestic labor force. The evidence appears to support that position. In reality, the U.S. trade deficit is a misleading number, too often used to stir protectionist attitudes. Various economists have noted that Great Britain ran a trade deficit for 200 years, and it really did not matter. I don't believe that a trade deficit is of paramount significance to a nation that is a world power.

DOMESTIC SAVINGS

The macroeconomic models of John Maynard Keynes stress that consumption is the driving force behind economic growth. He believed if consumers save too much, it has a negative impact on the economy. Although I do not disparage the importance of consumer spending on the economy (it represents roughly two-thirds of GDP), I side with the more classical theories of Adam Smith, who maintained that if consumers save, they keep their money in banks, which then lend to those who do want to spend money on consumer goods. Either way, someone is spending.

The idea that consumer spending drives the economy is somewhat flawed. This is especially true if interest rates are low. The major change affecting the economy over the last quarter of the twentieth century was a transition from secular inflation to secular deflation. Inflation fosters inefficiency, while deflation forces efficiency and cost containment.

Some encouraging evidence points to Americans saving more now than in the past. With the first wave of the baby-boom generation approaching retirement and the increased cynicism concerning the likelihood of Social Security's survival, Americans are realizing the need to save for retirement. In fact, reports at year-end 1998 showed that 25 percent of households earning $10,000–$25,000 own equities, directly or through retirement plans. The number rises for those earning $50,000–$99,000—two-thirds—and climbs to 84 percent for those earning $100,000 or more.

Companies are encouraging their employees to take responsibility for their own retirement needs. Consequently, people are taking a greater interest in economic conditions that affect their retirement asset of choice: stocks. Because Americans on average are enjoying rising incomes, they have created a new savings trend. Economic statistics show that even though consumer spending has increased, that increase can be traced to higher incomes and prior savings. Further, I believe that the trend toward increased savings is a result of real wages improving. Essentially, because real wages stagnated during the 1970s and 1980s, Americans could not "afford" to save.

IMPROVING CASH FLOW

Americans are saving for retirement at record rates. Since the beginning of the 1990s, new inflows into mutual funds have increased dramatically. The portion of households investing in stocks and mutual funds, as shown in Figure 1-2, rose from 31.7 percent in 1989 to 37.2 percent in 1992. By 1997, that figure reached 57.5 percent and continued growing in 1998 to 59.8 percent.

An analysis of adjusted money supply, M3 (the broadest measure of money supply, including currency, checkbook money, savings, time deposits, and the financial instruments of large institutions), suggests that Americans are continuing to save at record levels. Figure 1-3 demonstrates the dramatic rise in Americans' savings rates.

FIGURE 1-2

U.S. Households Investing in Stocks and Mutual Funds

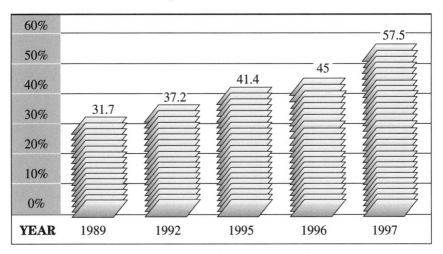

FIGURE 1-3

Domestic Money Supply Continues to Rise

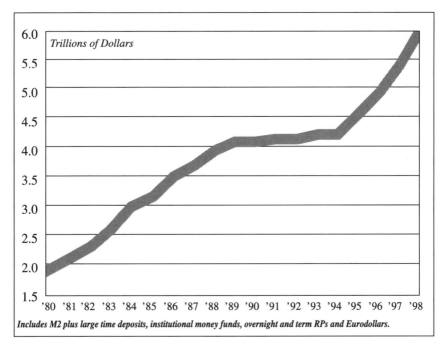

Includes M2 plus large time deposits, institutional money funds, overnight and term RPs and Eurodollars.

With savings comes the need to invest that capital. As Americans become more sophisticated in their personal financial management, they recognize the need to seek the greatest returns on capital available to them. In recent years, the stock market has largely been the vehicle of choice for the average American seeking a higher return on capital. As the volume of cash seeking higher returns increases, investors tend to bid prices up. Therefore, a liquidity premium is built into the price of an asset. As more cash becomes available to investors, they may bid prices up even higher.

Some economists fear this may lead to a speculative bubble and is often cited as the probable reason for the crash of the Japanese stock market's equivalent of the Dow, the Nikkei Index: too many yen chasing too few stocks. Furthermore, the speculative bubble fear may have contributed to the rapid decline in other markets in the middle of 1998 because investors more carefully examined the valuations on many of their assets. Ultimately, it is the underlying fundamentals of individual companies that drive the price of their securities. Market corrections, such as were seen during 1998, should not alarm investors. These periods of corrections are often good for the market, as they provide investors time to re-evaluate and adjust their portfolios.

I agree that pockets of speculative excesses in the market can exist. However, I believe that the fundamentals of the market justify the high valuations placed on securities. And the market's rapid recovery from 1998 corrections would seem to support this conclusion.

The United States is entering a unique period in its demographic makeup. Americans are recognizing the need to save more as they move closer to retirement. And these savings will seek a return in the capital markets. This trend alone should not be used as an indictment of the high valuations placed on securities.

I believe that there are strong fundamentals in favor of a stock market rising to Dow 40,000 by 2016. I am optimistic about the resurgence of the United States as an innovator, entrepreneur, and capitalist nation.

BALANCED BUDGET AGREEMENT

The effect that a balanced federal budget will have on the economy remains an area of speculation. Prior to 1998, the federal government had not run a surplus in three decades. However, the federal Office of Management and Budget (OMB) reported a unified budget surplus of $70 billion for 1998, and projected a 1999 unified budget surplus of $76 billion.

Economists constantly debate the significance of the federal budget deficit. Even the 1997 budget deficit of $22 billion represented a small part of an $8 trillion economy. Nonetheless, the projected surpluses should not necessarily absolve the federal government from making tough spending decisions. Congress and the President are fortunate, indeed, to have such a strong economy to bail them out of having to make difficult political decisions. However, in 1998, for the first time since the Nixon administration, the federal government ran a surplus. How will this affect the financial markets?

It seems rather obvious that the financial markets will view a balanced budget positively. Why this is so takes a little more explaining. Former Representative Mark Neumann (R) of Wisconsin explained the series of effects in the following manner, adapted from the *Congressional Record.*

1. Congress curtailed spending growth. That meant:
2. Less Washington borrowing. That meant:
3. More money available in the private sector. That meant:
4. Lower interest rates. That meant:
5. People bought more homes, cars, and other items. That meant:
6. More jobs created to build and assemble these products. That meant:
7. Fewer people on the welfare rolls and more taxpayers. That meant:
8. Much lower deficits. That meant:
9. The economy continued to grow.

Let's look at it another way:

1. Assume a fixed number of dollars to be invested in debt securities.
2. Assume the federal government issues no new government debt securities.
3. The number of bonds available for sale declines.
4. With the decreased supply of bonds, bond prices are bid up.
5. Interest rates come down.
6. Corporate debt becomes cheaper, and thus the overall cost of capital declines.
7. Businesses invest in more projects, thanks to the lower cost of capital.

8. Consumers increase consumption, especially of durable goods, because of lower interest rates.

9. The economy grows.

Both of these positions lead to the same conclusion: a strong economy. This naturally results in stronger corporate profits and increasing stock values. A balanced budget, if nothing else, will have a positive impact on stock values. The crux of the issue really is how the federal government spends its money. Unfortunately, balancing the budget has become an end unto itself.

If deficit spending will create future value greater than present value, it is not a bad thing. As much as a corporation borrows money to finance a worthwhile project so, too, the federal government could and should borrow money to finance worthwhile projects. The problem, of course, is that the federal government is generally inefficient and wasteful. Unfortunately, those individuals in power have shown that they cannot be trusted to make wise economic decisions. And unlike a business entity, the federal government can print its own money to pay off any obligations it cannot meet. It's more than likely that the private sector can undertake projects better and cheaper, and it is this rugged individualism that has built this country and will continue to see it to prosperity.

COOPERATIVE CENTRAL BANKING POLICIES

High growth and low inflation can, indeed, survive in the world at the same time. However, conditions must be appropriate to maintain this, among them productivity improvements and a pro-growth monetary policy. Inflationary pressures take over when labor markets tighten and current technologies are maximized. Proponents of the New Economy believe productivity improvements can continue. Because of increasing competitive pressures, firms will have no choice but to seek improved productivity in order to protect profit margins.

With the vast growth in technological advancements, the productivity cycle can continue longer than normal. The principles of classical economist Adam Smith support a harmony of low inflation and high growth rates. But the Keynes model, so prevalently used today, suggests that this is a difficult wedding of interests.

Consequently, it is important for whoever chairs the Federal Reserve Board to accept the notion of growth without inflation so that he or she does not interfere with the natural workings of the market. Federal

Reserve Board Chairman Alan Greenspan was accused of wandering from a pro-growth path because of his concerns about inflationary pressures. In 1998, the Fed, under Greenspan's guidance, lowered interest rates three times because of concern over a major worldwide slowdown. It may turn out that deflation, and not inflation, was the risk all along.

Current economic measures may not accurately reflect all components of the economy. I believe that the Consumer Price Index (CPI) number is inflated, which has a direct, negative effect on productivity measures. These small statistical discrepancies are significant because they have a major impact on Fed policy decisions. For example, higher productivity means that higher wages for workers are not as problematic as they would initially appear.

The silver lining to the economic chaos seen in Asia, Latin America, and Russia in 1998 was that more than 30 countries collectively lowered their interest rates 60 times. This showed worldwide cooperation and recognition by the world's central bankers and their governments that we truly are a global economy. Greenspan is known to have backed the New Economy paradigm among policy-makers. In the long run, Fed policies will probably lean toward a pro-growth agenda as political pressures often dictate.

CONCLUSION

In this chapter, I have established a base to launch the Dow to 40,000 by 2016. Economic fundamentals are as strong as ever. The basic tenets of the New Economy have entrenched themselves into the psyche of the economy. Based on very simple assumptions on future growth rates, Dow 40,000 is more of an inevitability than a bold prediction.

From its auspicious beginnings at the end of the nineteenth century, the Dow Jones Industrial Average has represented the best and brightest of America's businesses, evolving along the way into the measure most investors use to gauge market performance. Tables 1-3 through 1-8 present the Dow's highs, lows, and major moves over history.

One of the most significant reasons for my belief that the Dow's unrelenting advance will lead to 40,000 by 2016 is the changing economic landscape, unlike any seen in the twentieth century. In fact, the New Economy idea is heavily contingent on continued global growth and capitalization. New and expanding markets are opening their doors to the world, and investors will profit.

TABLE 1-3

Days with Greatest Point Gains				
Rank	Date	Close	Net Change	% Change
1	09/08/98	8020.78	380.53	4.98
2	10/28/97	7498.32	337.17	4.71
3	10/16/98	8299.36	330.58	4.15
4	09/01/98	7827.43	288.36	3.82
5	09/02/97	7879.78	257.36	3.38
6	09/23/98	8154.41	257.21	3.26
7	11/03/97	7674.39	232.31	3.12
8	11/23/98	9374.27	214.72	2.34
9	02/02/98	8107.78	201.28	2.55
10	12/01/97	8013.11	189.98	2.43

TABLE 1-4

Days with Greatest Percentage Gains				
Rank	Date	Close	Net Change	% Change
1	10/06/31	99.34	12.86	14.87
2	10/30/29	258.47	28.40	12.34
3	09/21/32	75.16	7.67	11.36
4	10/21/87	2027.85	186.84	10.15
5	08/03/32	58.22	5.06	9.52
6	02/11/32	78.60	6.80	9.47
7	11/14/29	217.28	18.59	9.36
8	12/18/31	80.69	6.90	9.35
9	02/13/32	85.82	7.22	9.19
10	05/06/32	59.01	4.91	9.08

TABLE 1-5

Days with Greatest Point Losses

Rank	Date	Close	Net Change	% Change
1	10/27/97	7161.15	−554.26	−7.19
2	08/31/98	7539.07	−512.61	−6.37
3	10/19/87	1738.74	−508.00	−22.61
4	08/27/98	8165.99	−357.36	−4.19
5	08/04/98	8487.31	−299.43	−3.40
6	09/10/98	7615.54	−249.48	−3.17
7	08/15/97	7694.66	−247.37	−3.11
8	09/30/98	7842.62	−237.90	−2.94
9	01/09/98	7580.42	−222.20	−2.85
10	11/30/98	9116.55	−216.53	−2.32

TABLE 1-6

Days with Greatest Percentage Losses

Rank	Date	Close	Net Change	% Change
1	10/19/1987	1738.74	−508.00	−22.61
2	10/28/1929	260.64	−38.33	−12.82
3	10/29/1929	230.07	−30.57	−11.73
4	11/06/1929	232.13	−25.55	−9.92
5	12/18/1899	58.27	−5.57	−8.72
6	08/12/1932	63.11	−5.79	−8.40
7	03/14/1907	76.23	−6.89	−8.29
8	10/26/1987	1793.93	−156.83	−8.04
9	07/21/1933	88.71	−7.55	−7.84
10	10/18/1937	125.73	−10.57	−7.75

TABLE 1-7

The Dow's Best Years			
Rank	**Date**	**Close**	**% Change**
1	1915	99.15	81.66
2	1933	99.90	66.69
3	1928	300.00	48.22
4	1908	86.15	46.64
5	1954	404.39	43.96
6	1904	69.61	41.74
7	1935	144.13	38.53
8	1975	852.41	38.32
9	1905	96.20	38.20
10	1958	583.65	33.96

TABLE 1-8

The Dow's Worst Years			
Rank	**Year**	**Close**	**% Change**
1	1931	77.90	−52.67
2	1907	58.75	−37.73
3	1930	164.58	−33.77
4	1920	71.95	−32.90
5	1937	120.85	−32.82
6	1914	54.58	−30.72
7	1974	616.24	−27.57
8	1903	49.11	−23.61
9	1932	59.93	−23.07
10	1917	74.38	−21.71

I see the introduction of the euro as Europe's single currency as nothing less than the genesis of the move to a single world currency. Within the first quarter of the twenty-first century, other single currency blocs will develop. The next bloc might be between the United States and Canada. I expect similar activity among the Asian nations, and a cooperative venture in Latin America.

As the world becomes more able to conduct business seamlessly from a currency standpoint, productivity will increase. And that prosperity will permeate the markets and reduce the risk of investing internationally.

CHAPTER 2

Global Growth and Capitalization

Since the end of the Cold War, markets previously unavailable to U.S. firms have opened their doors for business. In fact, since the mid-1990s, investment across borders has grown three times faster than world trade or world output. The global trend toward free markets, combined with stunning technological advances, has led to an international flow of funds.

Among world markets, one of the fastest growing is China. As China slowly opens its doors to foreign investors, a new untapped market of nearly 1.2 billion people becomes available. Although there have been some setbacks in Asian economies, these consumer markets represent incredible opportunities for American companies.

I compare the fallout from what happened to the economies in Asia, Latin America, and Russia in 1997 and 1998 with the fallout after the eruption of Mt. St. Helens. Once the volcanic dust settled, the land around Mt. St. Helens became more fertile, more productive. The economic aftermath for these nations will be similar; they are going to be more efficient, more prosperous, and better customers for America.

The westernization of Asia is only the beginning of the story of the world's changing economic fundamentals. Since the end of the Cold War, millions of consumers in former communist societies are creating new markets. In fact, in Latin America, strict adherence to market principles has put some countries on the fast track to economic health.

These new markets do present many challenges to investors, including political problems and possible capital shortages. In spite of the challenges, however, the world has entered the golden age of global economic expansion, and Corporate America is positioned to be a major beneficiary.

WHERE THE UNITED STATES STANDS

If history is a guide, the United States will supply both financial and physical resources, as well as technical expertise to emerging nations. American corporations are in a stronger economic position than their European counterparts, which continue to suffer under the weight of overbearing government, inflexible labor forces, and anemic economies.

American corporations have restructured and repositioned themselves to take advantage of the new economic landscape where information access and processing are the keys to success. For example, General Electric Chairman Jack Welch recognized opportunities in Asia and began 1999 with a new plan to accelerate GE's acquisitions and investments there as well as elsewhere around the world. Further, American industry is changing from a bloated bureaucracy to lean and mean management teams, from room-filling mainframe computers to laptops, from filing cabinets to cyberspace and the information superhighway. It is primed to take advantage of the new global economy.

According to *Business Week*'s list of the top 1,000 international firms, the United States accounts for roughly 50 percent of the roster's total market capitalization. American companies effectively dominate international trade, supplying customers with goods and services originating in the United States as well as other countries.

American firms can provide the products and services that developing economies want and need in the telecommunications, information technology, health care, and financial sectors. Consequently, I believe the United States is entering a golden age of exports. Since the economy is growing at a significant clip with low inflation, the prospects for American corporations look as bright as ever. Indeed, the United States already accounts for 25 percent of the world's production even though it makes up only 5 percent of the world's population.

In his book *The Coming American Renaissance,* Michael Moynihan outlines the United States' competitive advantages. Moynihan recognizes the abundant natural resources of the United States as a primary advantage. He points out that because the United States is bounded by two coasts, it allows the country to compete effectively in both the Pacific region of Asia and the Atlantic region of Europe.

Three times larger than the European Union, the United States is the fourth largest country in the world. Not only has its size led to a freedom of mobility, it prevents the development of rigid social hierarchies. In fact, 50 percent of the population moved between 1985 and 1989 and 90 percent since 1960.

The United States' vast history of discovery has produced a forward-looking culture, freeing the nation, as Moynihan states, from "the dead hand of tradition . . . In the United States, what you can do counts for more than who you are." No doubt, this is a country founded on risk taking. Americans are "fleeing taxes, unions, cities, and the aging buildings of the North for new construction down South . . . As Americans move in search of jobs, economic activity, or retirement, they generate other activity: the construction of malls, roads, and housing."[1]

Moynihan blames Europe's system of lifetime employment for perpetuating class differences. He notes that Americans change jobs, on average, about every two years, while the Japanese change jobs about every 30 years. While the European system of employment might guarantee a person a job, its famed apprenticeship system perpetuates class differences, is inherently inflexible, and predetermines what its members can achieve. This has had a negative effect on entrepreneurship, because individuals are conditioned to accept their lots in life.

Without entrepreneurship, European workers don't possess the enthusiasm to work the long hours that are customary of successful American workers. Further, Europe's heavy government regulations can extend the time required to obtain a corporate charter to six months, as compared with the United States' system where a corporate charter can be had via telephone, fax, or computer in a matter of minutes. Furthermore, technologically, the United States has a much higher educated workforce.

Things are beginning to change in Europe, however. The European marketplace is where the United States was in the 1980s, and more European companies are adopting American business practices, such as jettisoning weak divisions. Corporate layoffs and restructurings will

---

[1]Moynihan, Michael. 1996. *The Coming American Renaissance*. New York: Simon & Shuster, Inc., pp. 42, 96.

strengthen Europe's place as a world power. Consequently, Europeans will become great customers for the United States.

The spirit of entrepreneurship is gaining ground in European countries, where capital markets are beginning to think in terms of raising capital for new ventures. In 1997, European venture-capital firms raised $22 billion, more than double that raised the year before.

The United States not only enjoys the world's largest technology surplus, it runs the only technology surplus. Although chips and computers are manufactured globally, the concepts and designs are Silicon Valley's.

That the system of higher education in the United States is superior to that in most other countries is also a decided advantage. Approximately two-thirds of the world's top 100 universities are in the United States. Moreover, 66 percent of American high school graduates attend college, compared to 41 percent in other large member countries of the Organization for Economic Cooperation and Development (OECD). The United States devotes 6.6 percent of its Gross National Product (GNP) to education, ranking second among G-7 nations, after Canada at 7.2 percent. Japan, at 5.0 percent, is near the bottom but ahead of Italy at 4.8 percent.

If the American economy is shifting its focus from a capitalistic industrial economy to a knowledge-based service economy, as business scholar Peter Drucker believes, this distinction will rise in importance. The combination of these fundamentals serves as yet another justification for the expanding domestic equity market and for my confidence that the Dow will reach 40,000 by 2016.

CHINA AND THE ASIAN MARKETS

Asia and the Pacific Rim present intriguing investments. The region's 1997–98 economic upset can be likened to hitting a speed bump in the road. However, I believe that this area of the world economy will get its second wind and that within a few years, Asian markets will demonstrate their potential to return to high growth rates and to sustain them—for at least the next two decades. Also not to be overlooked is Asia's real GDP growth, which exceeded most of the industrialized nations' growth through mid-1997.

After the currency crisis in late 1997, growth stalled or was negative for much of the area, and Asian markets are only just beginning to assess the damage. Even though the International Monetary Fund (IMF) projected positive growth in the Asian markets for 1998 at 1.8 percent, this rate pales in comparison to the 8.2 percent and 6.6 percent growth rates enjoyed by the region in 1996 and 1997, respectively. Some individual countries, such as Malaysia and Thailand, have suffered disproportionately from the crisis and will face many challenges in the next few years in order to repair the damage.

Most important to recovery, these countries must reform their banking practices. Failed loans must be written off and stricter credit practices undertaken if they are to restore the confidence of capital markets. Only then will these regions regain the confidence of the foreign investors that they so desperately need in order to modernize their economies.

Despite the current problems of Asian markets, prior to the 1997 turmoil, China's stock market gained 40 percent in 1996. Thus, if Asian economies can be strengthened, there is little reason to doubt that a return to high growth rates in Asian stock markets may coincide with a recovery.

Those countries affected by the 1997–98 economic shake-up are taking appropriate action, even if it is at a slower than ideal pace, and it is this growth potential that will positively affect the American market. For example, Japan, which is expected to take the lead in the recovery process, has introduced its New Bridge Bank policy as its economic recovery starting point. A five-year plan, the bridge bank is charged with taking over failing banks and restoring appropriate accounting and credit practices.

Despite Asia's economic woes, it remains the largest untapped market in the world. As Asian governments slowly open their minds and their economies to Western economic ideas, these markets should eventually grow to the largest and most influential in terms of market demand.

Asia today is experiencing unprecedented change. For example, consider the major demographic shift of Asia's population. The lure of the opportunity to improve one's socioeconomic state in large cities is driving rural populations into cities at record numbers. This urbanization of Asia's population will stress the world's supply of natural resources and basic materials. According to the United Nations, Asia's urban population is projected to double from 1 billion to roughly 2.1 billion by 2020. This growth will require extensive infrastructure improvements to accommodate the increase in population, creating unparalleled opportunity for American firms capable of dealing with the needs of developing cities.

Infrastructure improvements are a vital component of continued economic expansion for developing nations. Improved infrastructure lowers transaction costs and improves the quality and efficiency of production, which eventually results in lower prices for goods and services. Ultimately, this will enhance Asia's competitive position in the global market.

Asia's growing need for infrastructure will, without a doubt, benefit those American companies that manufacture construction and materials handling equipment and capital goods equipment. For example, Caterpillar Inc., an American firm, sold $1.5 billion annually in tractors and earth-moving equipment in Asia. Other companies, such as John Deere & Co., will also have the opportunity to market agricultural equipment to the farming industry, and firms such as General Electric can offer its power-generation systems to electric utilities.

An example of the sheer magnitude of China's infrastructure needs is the telecommunications network. It has been estimated that China needs 114 million telephone lines to fulfill the expected increase in demand at a total cost of $100–$150 billion, roughly equivalent to recreating the United States or European telecommunications network.

World Bank estimates measure Asia's total infrastructure needs at close to $2 trillion by 2004, a feat nearly impossible to achieve. China alone is estimated to need $700 billion by 2004. Construction of the Three Gorges Dam along the Yangtze River, scheduled for completion in 2009 at an estimated cost in excess of $70 billion, is the largest project that China has undertaken in modern times.

An International Monetary Fund (IMF) report on the world economy pointed out that many developing countries continue to struggle with macroeconomic imbalances and structural impediments. With governments unable to meet their own infrastructure demands, analysts predict a boom for foreign companies working on build-own-transfer arrangements. These agreements call for a private firm to construct and finance a project, and then operate it until the project earns its predetermined rate of return before turning over operations to the local government.

American firms will, unquestionably, benefit from the construction windfall. Because of their competitive advantages, American companies will garner a disproportionate share of the orders for the capital equipment needed for infrastructure and telecommunications developments. Table 2-1 illustrates the significance of the present growth in Asia.[2]

---

[2]International Monetary Fund. 1998. "The Crisis in Emerging Markets—and Other Issues in the Current Conjuncture," *International Monetary Fund World Economic Outlook,* December, pp. 20, 25, 31, 32.

TABLE 2-1

Annual GDP Growth

	1996	1997	1998	Projections 1999
World output	4.2	4.1	2.0	2.5
Advanced economies	3.0	3.1	2.0	1.9
Major industrial countries	2.8	2.9	2.1	1.9
United States	3.4	3.9	3.5	2.0
Japan	3.9	0.8	−2.5	0.5
Germany	1.3	2.2	2.6	2.5
France	1.6	2.3	3.1	2.8
Italy	0.7	1.5	2.1	2.5
United Kingdom	2.2	3.4	2.3	1.2
Canada	1.2	3.7	3.0	2.5
Other Advanced Economies	3.8	4.2	1.4	2.3
Memorandum				
Industrial Countries	2.8	2.9	2.3	2.0
European Union	1.7	2.7	2.9	2.5
Euro area	1.6	2.5	3.0	2.8
Newly industrialized Asian economies	6.3	6.0	2.9	0.7
Developing countries	6.6	5.8	2.3	3.6
Africa	5.8	3.2	3.7	4.7
Asia	8.2	6.6	1.8	3.9
ASEAN-4	7.1	3.7	−10.4	−0.1
Middle East and Europe	4.7	4.7	2.3	2.7
Western Hemisphere	3.5	5.1	2.8	2.7
Countries in transition	−1.0	2.0	−0.2	−0.2
Central and eastern Europe	1.6	2.8	3.4	3.6
Excluding Belarus and Ukraine	3.7	3.2	3.7	4.1
Russia	5.0	0.9	−6.0	−6.0
Transcaucasus and central Asia	1.6	2.1	4.1	3.8
World Trade Volumes (goods and services)	6.8	9.7	3.7	4.6
Imports				
Advanced economies	6.4	9.0	4.5	4.7
Developing countries	9.3	9.8	1.0	4.6
Countries in transition	10.0	8.2	3.5	3.5
Exports				
Advanced economies	6.4	10.3	3.6	4.2
Developing countries	8.8	10.9	3.9	5.5
Countries in transition	7.0	6.9	5.3	5.9
Consumer prices				
Advanced economies	2.4	2.1	1.7	1.7
Developing countries	14.1	9.1	10.3	8.3
Countries in transition	41.4	27.9	29.5	34.6

Indeed, Asia has serious structural problems, and those problems must be appropriately addressed in order for the region to return to the path of prosperity. There is no question that this presents opportunities for U.S.-based, multinational companies to acquire, partner, and invest in Asian companies at what amounts to "fire sale" prices. Asian companies need the infusion of capital, and U.S. companies stand to profit.

INDIA

Another major player among the Asian markets is India. Investments in India have several advantages over investments in China. Traditionally, India's democratic government has been relatively stable, as opposed to China's changing political landscape. While China's expected average economic growth of 8 percent exceeds India's 6 percent, the evidence suggests that when risk is considered, investors can expect a better return from India. Studies show that India ranks 5th for the lowest investment risk out of the 10 largest emerging markets. China, on the other hand, ranks second for the highest investment risk. And while China's government has resisted some foreign projects and even reneged on contracts with foreign countries, India's government has welcomed foreign companies with open arms.

As build-own-transfer arrangements are becoming vogue, India's government offers guarantees amounting to a 16 percent return to firms willing to build and operate power plants. Despite these positives for India, Ernst & Young found in a survey of company executives that more than 50 percent preferred China over India for investment. However, 90 percent of the survey respondents cited China's political uncertainties as their greatest concern.

Part of India's difficulty in attracting foreign investment is the many documented problems with its stock market. As with all small markets, lack of liquidity is troublesome. In fact, *Global Finance* found that fund managers rated India the most difficult market in which to trade. Compounding the liquidity issue is India's record of poor clearing and settlement, insider manipulation, regulatory restrictions, and lack of access.

Although these problems, along with fragile banking systems, are inherent in almost all of the stock markets of emerging nations, it appears they may be more severe in India. Aggravating these problems is strict regulation restricting foreign ownership of common stock beyond a specified ratio.

The secondary market gives investors the option to make investments in India by acquiring shares of firms already operating there, by forming strategic alliances, or by making outright acquisitions. Because

TABLE 2-2

India's Economic Growth

Real GDP Growth	1992	1993	1994	1995	1996	1997	1998
	4.8%	3.5%	5.8%	8.2%	7.5%	5.6%	4.8%

of the regulatory issues and general liquidity problems, this option may not always be viable. Table 2-2 illustrates India's recent economic growth, which explains investors' bullishness.

It is incumbent upon governments of emerging markets to ease regulatory burdens, allowing secondary markets to develop a better system of self-rule. In addition, in order to ease the fears of investors, government agencies must take appropriate actions when irregularities arise. As a rule, the governments take little action; they often treat abuses with a slap on the wrist or simply ignore them. Nonetheless, many investors are willing to accept the risk.

While China remains the favorite among investors, India is a viable option. Much like China, India needs significant infrastructure improvements. Evidence suggests that India's government is more open to American and foreign firms than China's.

A multitude of potential opportunities is available to American firms, increasing the potential to increase their growth rates and, therefore, the growth of the market in general. For example, an American toothpaste company is considering manufacturing in India. The plant needs electrical, transportation, and telecommunications systems in order to profitably produce and distribute its product to the 968 million members of India's population. If India makes the necessary investments in infrastructure, still more promising investment opportunities will become available for American firms.

A SHIFT IN POWER

Developing countries will have an impact not only on the world's economic landscape, but also on the world's political landscape. *The Economist,* in its report "War of the Worlds," extensively examined the implications of this new economic era, where the traditional economic powers of the world, such as the United States, Great Britain, etc., no longer have the clout to which they were accustomed.

Having the largest economy in the world has advantages. It assures military security, for example, and confers superior economic status in dealing with other nations. It is a virtual certainty, however, that China will eventually be home to the largest economy in the world. With this increased economic power comes political power. The world is as close to resembling a single marketplace as it has ever been in history, and in order to continue this trend, it is important to continue to support the need for democratic reforms in emerging nations.

The benefits of free trade are well known. David Ricardo, a philosopher and economist, first introduced his theory of comparative advantage in the early 1800s. Basically, Ricardo's theory holds that the total output will be higher if each entity specializes in the field where it holds a comparative advantage. The point is that free trade provides more goods for households to consume, irrespective of the trading partners' status. Trade is not a zero-sum game. Industries that will prosper in the future will not be those shielded from the disciplines of foreign competition, but rather those that meet the challenge, and then lead the way.

A Canadian study by the Fraser Institute in Vancouver tied per capita income to economic freedom. Using a complex formula that took into account monetary policy and inflation, government operations and regulation, taxation and other appropriations, and restrictions on trade, the study found a close relationship between economic freedom and per capita income. At the top of the list was Hong Kong, followed by Singapore, New Zealand, and the United States. China received an "F" grade and was rated 81 out of 115 countries. Perhaps the secret to continued American economic superiority rests not with protecting what it has, but with constantly striving to be the world's freest economy, driven by personal innovation and entrepreneurship.

Most economists feel that the concerns of quickly losing power to China are unwarranted. China's 1998 growth rate was 7.8 percent, bolstered by massive government spending on public works projects. As China's economy becomes more mature, labor markets tighten, and actual GDP becomes closer to potential GDP, its growth will have to assume the more moderate rates seen in the present industrialized countries. How long this will take is speculation. I am confident that the United States will remain at the forefront of change.

Inevitably, China will pass the United States as the largest economy in the world, much as the United States passed Britain late in the nineteenth century. Some economists predict that by 2020, as many as 9 of the top 15 economies will emerge from the late twentieth century's Third World.

With the sheer number of people available for production jobs, the average Chinese individual's living standard may be much lower than

FIGURE 2-1

Global Population

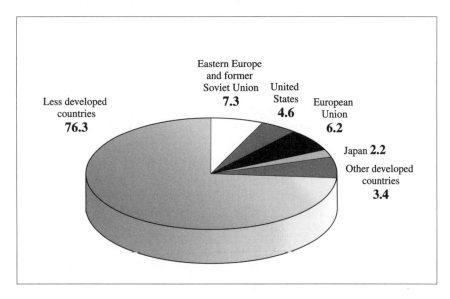

counterparts in the United States. But by virtue of its size, China's aggregate economy will exceed that of the United States. The upside is that the growth of developing economies will benefit the American economy, as exports increase along with the wealth of foreign countries. In fact, it is estimated that nearly half of all American exports today go to developing nations. Figure 2-1 illustrates the population disparity among regions and nations based on levels of economic development.

True growth, as demonstrated by the American economy, is strongest when accompanied by significant productivity improvements. China has a long way to go until its productive capacity is equal to American levels. A Fraser Institute study suggests that China will be significantly hindered until it is completely free of its communist system.

The quality of the free market instituted by the Chinese government has raised serious questions. Chinese banks are obligated to grant loans to less than qualified applicants if the business entities are state-owned or sponsored. As a result, a banking crisis already has struck China.

TRANSITION

During the transitional period of a truly global economy, political leaders will have to address the fundamental issues of low-skilled workers of industrialized nations being displaced because of the abundance of cheap, low-skilled labor available in developing nations. This adjustment may cause political tensions, which could cause a backlash toward foreigners and free trade.

Another concern is interest rates. Some economists warn that interest rates may rise because of the heavy investment needs of developing nations and the low supply of capital to fulfill those needs. Furthermore, the effect of adding 3 billion people to the world's economy will place pressures on inflation. There will be a raw materials and commodities shortage because of the growing demand for resources caused by an expanding economy.

The displacement of low-skilled workers in the United States has garnered much media attention because those most severely affected are those who can least afford it: low-skilled workers. There are several reasons to believe that the effect of this displacement will not be as severe as some may believe. Some of the lower-skilled and a portion of the unskilled will benefit from the United States' focus on education and training. These workers will have the opportunity to upgrade their skills to levels commanding higher compensation. As these newly trained workers move into higher-paid positions, they will reduce the labor pool at the lower levels, creating opportunities for low- and unskilled workers to fill jobs that still need to be done.

Government at various levels and the private sector have compiled a commendable record of cooperation in developing and conducting training programs to prepare workers. The welfare-to-work movement highlights the cooperative efforts in job training and skill enhancement. In a two-pronged effect, welfare-to-work has responded to the need for trained employees and has lowered the public-assistance rolls. Former welfare recipients, some of whom had looked upon public assistance as virtually a way of life, are enjoying a new level of self-worth, and the tax-paying public is enjoying lowered demands on its earnings and resources.

That American workers are far more productive than Third-World workers is partial justification for Americans' higher wages. Even after modern technology reaches developing nations, any productivity improvements without a corresponding real wage increase will cause a current-account surplus in Third-World nations. This will eventually lead to those countries' currencies appreciating and, thus, the effect will be nil.

There is a trend away from unskilled labor and toward high-skilled labor in the United States. The growth in demand for highly skilled labor has outpaced all other segments of the labor market in the United States.

There is an increasing disparity in compensation between high- and low-skilled labor. Analysts hold that the costs of capital, research and development, and marketing are more important factors in business decisions than are labor costs. This suggests that firms would not move out of the country simply because of cheaper labor. The reason that manufacturing jobs suddenly have become high paying and desirable is that there are fewer around and they are more demanding in terms of education and skill level.

In some industries, the role that labor plays in producing an item has fallen to the point that wages cannot justify the inventory costs, let alone transportation costs. When I visited a coal mine in Galatia, Illinois, for example, I quickly learned that the mining industry has advanced from picks and shovels to highly technical, satellite-guided digging and drilling. Now that the bulk of this mining company's work is performed using technology, its workers have to be more skilled in order to be employed there.

There is no such thing as low-skilled and high-paying manufacturing jobs. Frankly, people are paid what they are worth, and that is the value that they produce. In today's competitive global economy, business needs skilled and productive workers in order to profit from the global opportunities that opened with the end of the Cold War. Successful companies realize that they will be more profitable if they improve, rather than exploit, the capacities of their workers. Labor and management have probably never been more cooperative in American history.

THE ROLE OF INTEREST RATES

We know that infrastructure improvements in developing nations will require massive investments from wealthier nations to finance the projects, thereby putting stress on the world's supply of funds and raising interest rates. As there is need for additional capital to finance these projects, lenders will need to offer competitive interest rates in order to attract capital to the projects that they are financing.

During the late nineteenth century, the British provided much of the capital needed to help finance the infrastructure projects of the developing nations of the day, such as the United States and Argentina, without significantly raising interest rates. However, because of high government spending as well as significant public pension programs, which may discourage citizens from saving for retirement, there is concern that this time a capital shortage will cause a rapid increase in interest rates. I do not think this will happen for several reasons.

First, demographic changes suggest that Americans will save at much higher rates over the next 30 years because of the approaching retirement of the first wave of baby boomers. In addition, it is expected that higher incomes in developing nations will lead to higher savings by the citizens of those nations; thus, domestic financing is likely. Finally, the trend toward privatizing government pension programs could open a huge resource of capital previously unavailable to help finance these projects.

Whether all of these variables will be enough to satisfy the capital needs is yet to be seen. However, Adam Smith believed that the market's "invisible hand" in the long run will adjust for discrepancies. The market offers a powerful incentive for profit-motivated entrepreneurs. Smith's invisible hand theorizes that the advantage of capitalism corrects these types of problems. Whether energy, food, or capital shortages, if there are profits to be made, entrepreneurs will take steps to alleviate the problem.

Throughout the history of free markets, pundits have fretted over potential shortages of one vital resource or another. Yet with amazing consistency, markets have responded with new products and systems to meet demands. The problem with many of the economic models advanced by pessimistic, doomsday economists is their failure to consider the optimistic human spirit. More specifically, they forget to account for the entrepreneur, the very backbone of technological advance. As the motive increases to counter the shortages of resources, I believe that new systems will be created that will more efficiently use those on hand, and I am confident that the markets will respond again.

Currently, because of the abundance of resources, there is little profit motive to create more efficient systems. However, if and when there is a demand for alternative resources, history suggests that profit-motivated producers will step forward. During the OPEC oil embargo of the mid-1970s, for example, entrepreneurs turned to developing such alternative energy sources as solar, geothermal, and wind. Those innovators were driven by the opportunity to produce energy at costs below the record levels of oil prices. Interestingly, a strain on natural resources and commodities and the ensuing drive to solve its quandary will play to the American economy's strengths.

When the profit motive faces impediments, the entrepreneurial urge is stifled. Some economists, for example, feel that the federal government is artificially keeping the lid on the number of farmers in the United States through price controls, essentially weakening the profit motive. If American farmers are to share in the country's growing prosperity, they must be allowed to compete in a free market. Current government subsidies and supply controls insulate farmers from the disciplines of competition. In one survey, a majority of farmers favored a new system, apparently recognizing that their own survival depends upon it.

The United States will be at the forefront of technological research into maximizing current as well as creating alternative resources.

THE END OF THE COLD WAR

The end of the Cold War left the citizens of many former communist countries confused and uncertain about their futures. Political leaders, unfamiliar with Western economics, may have exacerbated an already problematic situation. Even after reforms were instituted, people distrusted the new economic system. For example, the former Soviet Union, which gained most of the news media attention. The collapse of the Russian economy bears remarkable similarity to the Asian crisis. Corrupt accounting practices, poor lending standards, political instability, and general confusion about a market economy created a difficult environment for reforms to take hold.

The world community and the Russian government must see that reforms take root and allow a new paradigm to take effect. Once that occurs, a boom similar to Asia's comeback should follow. From a world point of view, the success of the free market economy in the former Soviet Union will deeply affect millions of Russians, as well as the peace and security of countries around the world. Russia must take several steps in order to successfully shift to a market economy, such as smaller government, increased privatization, and incentives for international trade.

Those former communist countries that have introduced stable, open, and market-oriented policies have benefited the most, such as the Czech Republic. Russia must pursue such forward-thinking policies despite its setbacks in moving to a market-based economy, if it is to prosper.

After initial hardship, transition nations now show signs of life. The former Soviet Union has privatized more than three-quarters of the medium to large firms, which account for nearly 90 percent of its industrial production. Lamentably, only one-third of its workers are employed in the private sector.

A 1997 IMF World Report indicated several conditions necessary for transition economies to achieve a breakthrough. The recommendations include reducing inflation to reasonable levels, undertaking infrastructure improvements, and imposing capitalism on companies in the region. The hoped-for effect is that these countries will rise to the challenge of market pressures by improving their productive activities.

The report is optimistic about the chances of these countries achieving a full transition because of the region's high quality of education. The report suggests that in terms of human capital, transition countries may enjoy a comparative advantage. However, the report does point to the aging of the population as a possible obstacle.

Raymond Vernon of Harvard University's Kennedy School of Government suggests that there is no system for tackling the challenge of constructing a capitalist market for transition economies. He believes the type of market economy is often dependent upon the culture of the region. For example, some market economies have significant government involvement, as in Denmark and Sweden, where government disposes of about 50 percent of income. In addition, some market economies more closely resemble laissez-faire markets, such as the United States. Vernon uses the differences between Germany's and the United States' economies to exemplify this dynamic.

The American economy was shaped by the experience of its founders, who had great distrust of strong central governments. In the United States, "The entrepreneur was the hero," Vernon writes. This contrasts with the German experience, where as latecomers to the industrial movement in the nineteenth century, "German policymakers promoted the concept that workers and their employers were 'social partners' sharing in the benefits to be generated by their enterprises."

While refraining from judging one system superior to another, Vernon does point out that the American system enjoys greater flexibility, giving firms, "The ability . . . to restructure their workforces, abandon some installations and relocate others as changing technologies have required." Vernon concludes that this gives "U.S. firms a new edge in international competition."[3]

It will be interesting to see the system that the states of the former Soviet Union adopt. In a gathering of G-7 leaders where Russia was added as the eighth member, President Bill Clinton did his best job of selling the American form of capitalism. Shifting completely to the American model of a capitalist society will prove difficult for transition countries, because their citizens have been entrenched in a communist system for decades upon decades. The effect that this cultural phenomenon will have on the citizens as they adapt to the free market is yet to be seen.

---

[3]Vernon, Raymond. 1996. "Constructing a Market Economy: A Guide for Countries in Transition," *Economic Reform Today* (Number 2): 4–5, Center for International Private Enterprise, Washington, D.C.

Initial attempts at privatization ostensibly failed because programs were designed with the expectation that the citizens would react as Americans or Europeans would when incentives were provided. They did not. One such example was the government-created employee ownership plan, which was to allow private ownership of formerly public enterprises. In Russia, many citizens did not understand the process and, consequently, did not participate. Those who received shares were more concerned with their jobs than with their equity. As a result, they did not give full effort to the privatization movement. The implication is that the culture of communism may have to die before permanent progress can be made.

Other reasons beyond cultural led to the initial failure of capitalism in the former Soviet Union. Former officials became managers of newly privatized firms. Many of these managers exploited the general population and desperately tried to maintain their social status through whatever means necessary.

Abuses of power during the transition to a market economy are well documented. Among them were intimidation of employees and total disregard or manipulation of new laws and regulations. Management often would force employees to surrender their ownership shares to management at prices far below market value or be threatened with job termination, all of which helped keep shares in the hands of insiders who purportedly understood the company better. Many managers never seemed to grasp the discipline of free markets, often clamoring for some sort of central planning to control survival-threatening problems instead of creating innovative solutions.

Insiders resisted the assistance of outsiders, particularly foreigners who wanted to restructure the firms in exchange for their capital. Insiders saw outsiders as profiteers, not motivated by the firm's best interests. As a result, insiders developed unethical means of keeping outsiders out. One such tactic was to dilute shares purchased by outsiders by issuing new shares to friendly investors at prices far below market prices. Without corporate governance laws, little could be done to combat the unethical and borderline illegal behavior.

Attempts at alleviating the problem largely failed, as new laws were simply ignored or manipulated to benefit the status quo. The effect of this behavior has been to slow progress, as numerous outsiders with capital, which firms desperately need to restructure their operations, invested elsewhere. Despite all of these problems, as well as a history of central planning, some evidence suggests that an American form of capitalism is

TABLE 2-3

The Russian Economy

	1991	1992	1993	1994	1995	1996	1997	1998E
GDP	−12.8%	−18.5%	−12.0%	−15.0%	−9.0%	−5.0%	.9%	−6.0%
CPI	+138	+2,323	+844	+202	+131	+48	+15	+48
Unemployment	NA	4.9	+5.5	+7.1	+7.9	9.3	NA	NA

E–estimated
NA–Not Available

dominating the new economic landscape, and the spirit of entrepreneur-ship has not been lost in the former Soviet Union.

In the early years of the newly formed Russian Federation, the number of private and privatized enterprises grew almost fourfold. The fastest growth rate came in 1991 and 1992 when the number of small start-up, private, and privatized enterprises more than doubled. The number of small start-ups by the end of 1995 reached an estimated 795,000.

The Eastern bloc will be dominated by the Russian Federation. In and of itself, Russia represents the world's largest country in terms of land mass. Its population is nearly 150 million, and it is by far the strongest industrial nation of the former Soviet Union. Unlike China, Russia is rich in natural resources, much as Latin America is. Unfortunately, toward the end of the communist regime this led private "entrepreneurs" to take advantage of grossly underpriced commodities and weak border controls.

One example of exploitation is refined oil, which sold for 146 times more on world markets than in the Soviet Union. A person could buy or skim off refined oil, smuggle it across a border, and become rich overnight. The result was that totally unprepared Russian consumers faced overnight hyperinflation after market rates were adopted.

Political and economic events led to the collapse of the Russian economy. As Table 2-3 shows, the Russian economy was beginning to turn around over the last decade. The Russian stock market, in terms of U.S. dollars, rose 124 percent in 1996 and continued its rugged pace in 1997, lunging forward 105 percent before collapsing under the weight of political instability and market corruption in the latter part of 1997.

The Russian market lost 80 percent of its value in 1998. If that market is to regain any momentum, it will be imperative that true market reforms be implemented. In the same time frame that many emerging markets were falling apart, the U.S. stock market powered to new records, driven by the strength of the U.S. economy. Irrespective of developments in emerging markets, the United States continued to prosper economically.

THE CZECH REPUBLIC

The Czech Republic is considered the star of all transition countries, holding many advantages over the other transition countries. Czech citizens are committed to political and economic reforms, while the Russian people have resisted reforms, most likely because of lack of understanding about their implications. Further, in the Czech Republic, private activity accounts for roughly three-quarters of the GDP, and thanks to a surplus in tax revenues, the government is contemplating restructuring the tax system, considered the highest in the region.

While political instability has led to problems in Hungary and Poland, the two other most advanced economies in Eastern Europe, economic growth in the Czech Republic has hovered around 3 percent. Not astounding, but solid. Combined with an extremely low unemployment rate, the Czech Republic has the best macroeconomic fundamentals of all the transition countries.

The Czech Republic faces several challenges, however. The central bank has pursued a tight monetary policy in order to control inflation. The koruna, the Czech currency, proved to be overvalued because of a rising current-account deficit. Consequently, in April 1997, the currency was revalued. Much as in Russia, larger industries deemed important have yet to be privatized, although some believe that the Czech Republic is very close to doing so. Smaller firms also need to be restructured to take advantage of potential productivity improvements.

To this point, the strong currency has allowed firms to keep wages artificially low. When the currency is revalued, wage rates will rise and businesses will have to lay off some employees and replace their productivity with capital. However, the increase in output needed for the increase in exports should eventually make up for any unemployment.

Much of the success of the Czech Republic's economy is due to the government's encouragement of foreign participation without discrimination. That is in direct contrast to Russian businesses, which have gone to great lengths to contest foreign influence. The method of privatization used by the Czech Republic is similar to that of Russia. Both used the voucher system, under which citizens received vouchers or bought them at discounted rates. The vouchers were then exchanged for shares of stock in formerly public firms.

In Russia, the voucher system was completely misunderstood. Managers literally duped citizens into selling their vouchers at deep discounts or face persecution. In the Czech Republic, investment funds were created to manage the vouchers. Nearly two-thirds of the citizens invested in these funds, placing a great deal of pressure as well as power in the hands of the investment fund managers. That was the citizens' first opportunity to earn a profit after 50 years of state control.

The power of these trusts concerns many who notice that the top four Czech investment funds hold approximately 80 percent of the shares of private firms, the highest concentration of ownership in any market economy. The funds are run by former state bankers, considered to be heavily influenced by government forces.

While there is a law against any fund owning more than 20 percent of a single firm, there is no law prohibiting collaborative efforts of funds to influence corporate policy, which has created a conflict of interest. Banks oppose the funds' engaging in dramatic downsizing or restructuring or initiating bankruptcies because of the risk of loan defaults.

Czech fund managers are compensated according to the size of a fund instead of its performance. Therefore, a further concentration of business is likely. Naturally, the concern is that the restructuring of firms, which needs to take place, will be delayed because of the conflicts of interest. It is reported that state ownership of banks in the Czech Republic has had a detrimental effect on the management of the investment funds. The end result, nevertheless, is that the average Czech citizen has become an owner.

It is expected that privatization will continue and that foreign investments will flow into Czech capital markets. While there is concern about the growing power of investment funds, government regulation and foreign competition are expected to eventually hinder any monopolistic activity.

The key to success in Eastern Europe will be private ownership, a stable monetary environment, low taxes, and freedom of exchange. The positive correlation between economic growth and economic freedom suggests that countries that follow policies more consistent with economic freedom reap a harvest of more rapid economic growth, which leads to higher living standards. Thus, Eastern European countries must continue to strive toward extending economic freedom to their citizens in spite of initial hardships.

A successful economy abroad means more opportunity at home. The growth and success of Eastern-bloc nations can only translate into good things for the United States, among them Dow 40,000 by 2016.

LATIN AMERICA

The emerging markets in Latin America will also enjoy rapid growth over the next 20 years, providing opportunity for American corporations and individual investors. With a wealth of natural resources and a market base of 400 million people, Latin America is the second-fastest-growing region in the world. While Latin America's growth is less dramatic than that in Asia, its countries' more disciplined adherence to free market principles, as well as their democratic forms of government, may convince many investors to look south for opportunities. Such economic reform measures as privatization initiatives, stable currencies, declining inflation rates, and a rebound in real growth have added to Latin America's appeal for foreign investors.

One blemish on the Latin American record was the 1995 general economic downturn. However, beginning in 1996, the seven major economies of Latin America grew an average of 4 percent annually in the following two years. Table 2-4 shows GDP growth for some Latin American countries as well as for the region as a whole. Further, inflation appears to have been brought under better control, as the inflation rate was expected to decline to 10.8 percent in 1998, down from 23 percent in 1996, which may be due to significant improvements in monetary and exchange rate policies in Mexico and Venezuela.

TABLE 2-4

Latin America GDP Growth

	1994	1995	1996	1997	1998E
Brazil	5.7%	4.2%	3.0%	2.8%	4.0%
Mexico	2.5	−6.2	5.1	5.2	4.5
Latin America	4.7	−0.1	3.5	5.1	2.8

E–estimated

Mexico has announced a goal of 5 percent economic growth with overall investment at 25 percent of GDP by 2000. However, high unemployment remains a problem in much of the area, but the trend should reverse.

Latin America remains committed to privatization. Chile's private pension plan has been well documented and consistently commended by free-market economists as proof that the market works better than government. Privatization of utilities and banking is also on target and it appears that this will bring even more stability to the area. The trend toward privatization in these areas has increased private investment relative to public investment.

Much like East Asia and Eastern Europe, Latin America also faces many challenges. Sustaining economic growth in light of negligible savings rates will be one challenge. Latin American savings rates are about 19 percent of GDP compared with the emerging market average of about 35 percent. Other challenges include continuing liberalization of trade. One great success story is that of Mercosur, a regional trade agreement among Argentina, Brazil, Paraguay, and Uruguay. The World Bank calls it one of the more successful trade agreements in the region, if not in the developing world as a whole. This free-trade agreement has done on a smaller scale what is now in process in Europe with the advent of the curo.

Exports also are surging, expanding at an average rate of 10 percent. Continued productivity improvements through improved infrastructure and higher quality standards must also become a priority.

Latin America has succeeded in changing its political structure, providing a more stable political environment. In the previously cited study dealing with investment risk in emerging markets, Argentina and Mexico ranked first and third, respectively.

Latin America has made conscious efforts to improve relationships with industrialized nations, thus endearing itself to the international community. Latin American countries understand that they will have growing involvement in international affairs as their economic size and stature grow. They recognize that they will need foreign investment to help build their infrastructures as well as improve economic opportunities in the region.

Just as in Asia, Latin American countries must make infrastructure improvements if they are to reach their full productive potentials. In fact, Latin America and Asia may be competing for the same capital, with the winner in this game quickly asserting itself as the economic heavyweight. Latin America appears to be winning. Excluding China, in 1996, Latin

America had more direct foreign investment than Asia, with $25.9 billion of inflows compared to $18.8 billion for Asia.

One of the big winners in the contest for foreign investors is Argentina, which may be due to its answering the challenge of infrastructure improvements. Specifically, improvements in its highways, ports, and waterways are lowering transportation costs and helping to improve its production capabilities. For example, the upgrading of the Buenos Aires port structure through private investment decreased the average time to handle a vessel from 72 hours to 12 hours, a significant improvement in productivity. This improvement should be reflected in lower prices, thus keying an improved competitive position.

Another challenge in Latin American countries will be alleviating severe poverty and inequality among citizens, which the World Bank calls the Achilles' heel of the region. The World Bank estimates that 25 percent of the population lives on less than $1 per day. The solution requires extending job opportunities to many of the urban poor, which may include improving education through investment in human capital. Unlike in Eastern Europe where a significant portion of the population is well educated, the average adult in Latin America has 5.2 years of education, two years less than the average for markets at similar stages in development.

Finally, as is the case throughout the world, the governments of Latin America must perform more efficiently. That will mean reformed public finance, effective legal oversight, and improved government services.

CONCLUSION

In a global market, good fortunes for countries abroad means good fortunes for the United States. As emerging nations become richer, American exports rise, products become cheaper, and in general, standards of living increase everywhere. That does not even take into account the heavy direct involvement that American firms will have in the infrastructure construction. All of these variables bode well for moving the stock market toward Dow 40,000 by 2016.

Free trade is not something to be feared, but a celebration of a new global economy. While the transition will not be easy or without rough spots, setbacks will be temporary. The end of the Cold War has allowed many nations to divert resources from military budgets into more productive areas, such as quality of life or research and development spending.

The global financial crisis of 1997–98 may have been, in effect, a kind of blessing. It focused world fiscal experts on the weaknesses in the global system and allowed them to develop procedures designed to lengthen the wave of global expansion and reduce dramatic swings.

The crisis may have ushered in an age of cooperation unlike any seen before.

Just as the dropping of the atomic bomb and the resulting fear of nuclear weapons kept countries from using them for many decades, fear of a financial meltdown, which the world almost experienced in 1998, may prevent one for decades.

Free trade will be good for Wall Street, and for Main Street. The world is embarking on a New Economy. International competition will keep inflation low, overseas markets will boost sales, and new information industries will drive exports. Economic growth, along with curbs on government spending and taxation, will lead to lower interest rates and an increased supply of capital.

The emergence of Darwinian capitalism in Asia represents another major change in the basic rules of business. While this form of capitalism is new to the Asian economies, it is well known in the United States. The strongest companies with the best products, management, and entrepreneurial vision will thrive in this environment.

As Asia incorporates fundamental changes, the transition period undoubtedly will be characterized by volatility in Asian capital markets. As the impact of the Asian crisis on U.S. markets unfolded, opportunities arose. This connection is appropriately seen in the written Chinese language, where the illustration of crisis includes opportunity.

Recall the Latin American crisis of 1994–95. The Mexican Bolsa fell 50 percent in the first six months, but then rebounded 83 percent from the low just 12 months after the bottom. Over the same time, the United States market gained slightly in the first six months, but followed that by gaining 36 percent over the next 12 months. The world is at the dawn of a new era, one which should excite both new and seasoned investors.

CHAPTER 3

Social Security, Economics 101, and a Booming Economy

This chapter provides an unvarnished view of Social Security and how it looms imposingly over retirement planning efforts. Not too long ago in Washington, the very idea of privatizing Social Security was a kind of blasphemy. Social Security was untouchable in American politics. Any politician who suggested serious changes was, more often than not, looking for a new job following the next election.

One of the last bastions of pure socialism, liberal economists and politicians alike desperately held to the belief that the Social Security system truly was big government at its best. No project in the history of this country has done more to redistribute wealth than Social Security. Done under the guise of taking care of the elderly, Social Security was certainly a noble intention. Unfortunately, the creators of this system failed to anticipate the potentially backbreaking effects it could have on the economy.

The original intention of Social Security was to serve as a supplement to retirement income, not to be the sole source of income. Unfortunately, Social Security has created zero incentive to save. For example, those who properly prepared for retirement by saving and investing and now enjoy a decent income stream are penalized through taxation of their Social Security benefits. Social Security contributions are not supposed to be simply another income tax, as they are generally viewed, but rather savings for retirement. It was only a matter of time before someone discovered a better way.

In this chapter, we'll examine the state of the Social Security system, look at its problems, and describe and analyze some of the solutions proposed by various politicians and economists, because all of these issues tie into Dow 40,000 by 2016. We'll also look at why the system has failed and whether it can be saved while creating unparalleled wealth and opportunity for American citizens. Given the success of privatization initiatives in other countries dealing with programs similar to Social Security, we'll also examine whether similar moves can work in the United States.

ECONOMICS 101

In Steven Landsburg's book *The Armchair Economist,* he writes, "Most of economics can be summarized in four words: 'People respond to incentives.' The rest is commentary." And you thought economics was difficult. The point is that almost any activity is motivated by some incentive, economic or otherwise. To suggest the contrary is to demonstrate an inability to accept human nature.

To illustrate his point and to show that incentives aren't always economic (even though they may have an economic consequence), Landsburg uses several very powerful examples to illustrate that people respond to incentives. He begins with the notion that seat belts kill. Although it seems easy to dismiss this argument as ludicrous or inane, further investigation produces a surprising result.

First, an examination of the resulting incentives needs to be identified. In this case, there is an incentive to drive less carefully because the risk of dying in an automobile accident is lower when wearing a seat belt. Citing a study conducted in the 1970s by Sam Peltzman, Landsburg concludes, "There were more accidents and fewer driver deaths per accident, but the total number of driver deaths remained essentially unchanged." In crude terms, the market had determined that a certain number of deaths in car accidents was acceptable and, therefore, drivers will adjust their behavior accordingly.

Further, psychologists have found that when someone is handed an unexpectedly hot cup of coffee, typically the cup is dropped if it is perceived to be inexpensive, but the individual hangs on if the cup is believed to be valuable.[1] The point is that incentives do matter, especially eco-

---

[1] Landsburg, Steven E 1995. *The Armchair Economist.* New York: Simon & Schuster, p. 8.

nomic ones. And in the case of Social Security, unfortunately, a negative incentive has been created.

NEGATIVE INCENTIVES DEPRESS SAVINGS

There has been a shift from viewing Social Security as supplementary income for retirees to a view that Social Security benefits are fundamental to survival. Many retired individuals will confess that Social Security is their very lifeblood. Their incentive to save for retirement was absent in light of their belief that Social Security would take care of them. Further, saving for retirement essentially resulted in forfeiting one's Social Security benefits by virtue of higher marginal tax rates, which should be the individual's property. However, a 1960 Supreme Court decision ruled that workers do not have any accrued property rights associated with Social Security.

The World Bank has concluded that Social Security undermines savings. This dynamic has been seen at work in policy decisions regarding education and housing, where because of subsidies, savings for these purposes have dwindled. In the United States, studies show that savings are reduced by 60 cents for every dollar of perceived payments in Social Security. This disincentive to save has a negative impact on the economy. Research indicates that the economy underperforms by as much as 1 percent annually because of the current payroll tax obligation, discouraging both the quantity and quality of employment. That amounts to approximately $85 billion per year in underperformance, or approximately $1,000 per family of four.

We've already considered the power of compound interest, so imagine the cumulative negative effect of this policy. In the 20 years leading up to 2016, a 1 percent drag on the Gross National Product (GNP) will amount to $150 billion. Conversely, the Chilean experience, discussed in more detail later, has shown that savings increased by 150 percent during the 1980s after the country's private system was initiated in 1981.

The very fact that individuals invest in stocks further proves that people respond to incentives. Stocks allow for some deferment of taxes, which increases the after-tax return. When stocks are sold, they are taxed at the capital-gains rate, often less than the income tax rate an individual would otherwise have faced.

SOCIAL SECURITY SOLVENCY

The disincentives that Social Security creates are just one part of the problem with the current system. Social Security is going broke. Social

Security ran about a $100 billion surplus in 1998, but beginning in 2012, it will begin running in red ink. In today's dollars, this unfunded liability is estimated to be between $9 trillion and $12 trillion. Even the Social Security trust fund cannot save the current system, as it will keep the system solvent only until 2032. At that point, inflows to the system will cover only 75 percent of outgoing benefit payments. Figure 3-1 illustrates Social Security's effect on the federal budget.

With baby boomers rapidly approaching retirement age, it is imperative that two things occur. First, Social Security must be revamped. The pay-as-you-go system was doomed from the beginning, reminding some economists of a grand pyramid scheme. Social Security has been described as a Ponzi scheme that relies on increasing the number of people putting money into the pot, which is then used to pay off earlier participants. The result is an illusion of a return on investment. Ponzi schemes work only if more people are "suckered" into the game. The problem with Social Security is that we're running short on suckers, as Fig. 3-2 clearly illustrates.

Birth rates in the United States have been rapidly decreasing while life expectancy rates has been increasing. In the 1940s, 1950s, and 1960s, women averaged 2.5 children each. The average woman now bears two

FIGURE 3-1

Social Security's Effect on the Budget

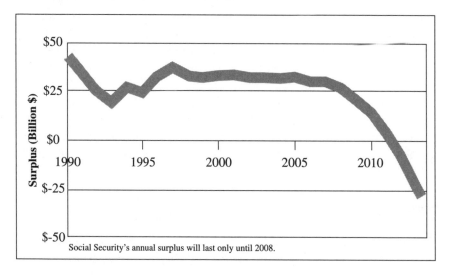

Social Security's annual surplus will last only until 2008.

FIGURE 3-2

Workers Contributing for each Social Security Beneficiary

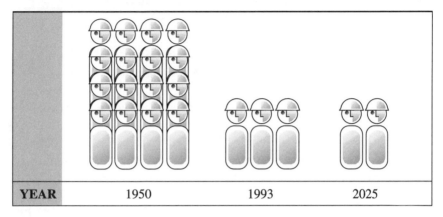

| YEAR | 1950 | 1993 | 2025 |

children, and the average rate is expected to continue to fall. Furthermore, the life expectancy in the 1930s was 65, as opposed to 75 at the end of the twentieth century. This graying of the population is a key factor in the battle for pension reform.

Public pension programs throughout the world are nearly broke. There will simply not be enough money in the programs to pay for the vast number of people about to retire. Japan, Italy, France, and Germany all face tough fiscal decisions because of pension programs that are driving them bankrupt. As a result, it is estimated that new contributors will see real annual rates of return of –2.5 percent to –3 percent on their Social Security contributions. That is only if the current system is able to stay solvent, which most likely would occur through increased payroll taxes, which would lower rates of return even further. Contrast that with current recipients who receive three to five times what they put into the system.

On average, only individuals born before 1926 are better off under the current system than if their Social Security payments had been invested in a mix of stocks and bonds and earned the market return over that time period. In fact, almost all current contributors under age 55 would do better if their payments between now and retirement had been invested in private retirement funds and earned the historical market return.

Social Security reinforces the disincentive to save and provides a poor rate of return. The system merely perpetuates the trend of redistribution of wealth, which I believe needs to be stopped in everyone's best interests. Supporters of the present system claim that annual productivity improvements of just 1 percent will solve the problem. They fail to realize that this is on top of Social Security projections, which already inhibit productivity improvements.

Adjusting for productivity or economic growth or any other assumption used in the projections, accurate or not, won't solve the true problem. While it may resolve the issue from a government fiscal perspective, it doesn't get at the crux of the issue: income redistribution, which benefits few.

The responsibility for funding retirement must be returned to the individual, which may mean privatizing the retirement system and making participants mandatory shareholders with shareholders' rights, of course, or simply eliminating mandatory retirement savings completely. I support privatization for several reasons, and Table 3-1 illustrates the cost of further delays.[2]

First, Social Security's problems should be addressed promptly and on a bipartisan basis. Second, solutions should work to increase individuals' savings rates. Third, individuals should have a wider range of choices for their savings.

TABLE 3-1

Cost of Delay to Implement Reforms
(Assumes No Change from Current System)

Implementation Date	Percent of Tax Necessary to Maintain Benefits at Current Levels	Percent of Benefit Cuts to Maintain Taxes at Current Levels
2002	20.16	20.5
2012	25.16	25.5
2022	32.58	33.5

---

[2]Mark E. Lackritz, president of Securities Industry Association, testimony before United States Senate Committee on Banking, Housing & Urban Affairs Subcommittee on Securities, Hearing on Social Security Privatization's Impact on the Stock Market, April 30, 1997.

Even the Social Security Administration estimates that payroll taxes will need to be increased to 28 percent (40 percent including Medicare) to close the gap between inflows and outflows. The ensuing negative impact on the economy could cost 3.5 million jobs, perhaps more when Medicare is added into the equation.

PRIVATIZATION: A TOUGH POLITICAL SELL

Despite all of these negative factors, there is fervent support in Washington for the archaic Social Security system. Solutions to save the system include raising payroll taxes, forcing all state and local government workers into the system, taxing Social Security benefits more harshly, scaling back the cost of living adjustments, requiring government-controlled investment of the trust fund, initiating means testing, and using price-indexing instead of wage-indexing to reduce the initial benefit amount. The problem with these solutions is that they simply decrease the already inadequate rates of return.

Means testing is effectively a tax on upper-income seniors. Means testing results in those who earn more than a certain level of income having their benefits reduced or eliminated. In effect, workers and seniors are being told not to work, not to save, and not to be responsible for funding their own retirements. If they do, they will face penalties. Increasing taxes hardly seems politically viable, considering that raising taxes didn't fix the problem the last time either.

There is a push in Congress to solve the problem by adjusting for changes in the cost of living. The federal government uses the Consumer Price Index (CPI) to gauge increases in federal benefits, primarily those that affect Social Security benefits and military pensions. Although it is generally accepted that the CPI is a poor measure of inflation, creating a new index only delays the problem of fixing the Social Security system and lowers the return on investment even further.

Still, the solution is popular among some politicians because it repairs the problem for a little while longer. The federal government can keep Social Security on the fiscal books and, thus, continue to take advantage of its surpluses to lower potential deficits. Business and management expert Peter Drucker refers to this practice of using public pension plans for political purposes as "looting." In *Post-Capitalist Society,* he writes that public pension plans "have regularly been misused to plug holes in the budgets of states and cities."[3] It truly is a case of accounting gimmickry and more smoke-and-mirrors government.

This does not mean that the CPI should not be changed. A new index would measure inflation better, taking into account changes in consumer buying patterns. This should not be used as a tool to fix a broken system, however. It's kind of like sticking gum on a water leak. While it may allay the problem for a while, eventually, the entire dike may break.

Even the famed 1997 federal balanced budget deal is seen by most economists as failing to address the core budget problem, that of spending. The budget deal was passed at the eleventh hour, thanks to some updated Congressional Budget Office statistics that showed that revenues were higher than anticipated, suggesting a faster growing economy than was expected.

Naturally, a stronger economy is positive. However, the key to fixing the budget's long-term problems lies in controlling spending. Adjusting the growth rate of entitlement spending to more accurately reflect inflation has long been a solution offered by Republicans to solve the entitlement problem. That approach is increasingly being accepted by Democrats, probably because of the near-crisis situation with entitlement spending. Nonetheless, it is a step in the right direction and, hopefully, fiscal responsibility is here to stay.

Unfortunately, the problem will eventually return. Instead of perpetuating the problem, we must work to solve it. According to some studies, privatizing Social Security contributions would result in retirement income from three to five times the present benefits. The power of compounding interest is again key. As Martin Feldstein, a Harvard University economist, suggests, smaller contributions of, for example, 2.5 percent of wages, growing at a rate of 10 percent per year, would exceed the value of a fund generated by a 12.5 percent-of-wages contribution in a non-interest-earning account.

Feldstein presents an even more compelling argument for privatization. He estimates that payroll taxes of just 2.5 percent, invested in private funds, would result in equal benefits produced by the current Social Security system, which imposes 12.4 percent payroll taxes.

---

[3]Drucker, Peter F. 1993. *Post-Capitalist Society.* New York: HarperCollins Publisher, Inc., p. 75.

INCENTIVES

According to several polls, increasing numbers of Americans ranging in age from 20 to 60 typically do not expect Social Security to be around when they reach retirement. What is disturbing, however, is that they apparently are doing nothing about it. Roughly half of those polled report that they have saved less than $10,000 for retirement.

In addition, the increases in debt accrual have added a second potential problem on top of the lack of savings: almost half of the survey respondents said that they regularly roll over debt on their credit cards. Finally, three-quarters acknowledge that they should be saving more for retirement. Consequently, the question that begs to be asked is: is this a violation of the incentive rule? Not necessarily. While it is possible that Social Security will not exist, for most Americans the reality hasn't set in. Nor, for that matter, has the impending certainty of retirement.

Interestingly, unlike baby boomers, individuals are almost twice as likely to have saved a nest egg in excess of $100,000 if they are pre-retirees in their fifties. That is a result of two phenomena, which support the principle that incentives matter. First, the older group has had a longer time to save and, thus, has gained on the time value of their money. If the assets of the younger group were projected for the time-value of money, the number of respondents with more than $100,000 in assets would approach or surpass the older group.

Second, people respond to incentives. As an individual approaches retirement, the incentive to save increases proportionately with age. Furthermore, because earnings typically peak during these pre-retirement years, individuals can afford to save more. Therefore, with the urgency of retirement, plus the increasing reality of a smaller safety net, savings will increase dramatically as people become better informed. As baby boomers reach pre-retirement age, savings should increase significantly. The federal government got involved in promoting savings when it passed the SAVER Act in 1997. The SAVER (Savings Are Vital to Everyone's Retirement) Act is a program designed to educate the public about the importance of savings. The act requires the Labor Department to maintain an ongoing education program that describes the types of retirement plans available, creates a means for individuals to calculate their retirement needs, and provides information to employers on retirement plans and how to implement them. It also requires a summit on savings, a type of forum sponsored by the federal government. Although the SAVER Act is a positive measure, it only informs the public about the dire need to save more for retirement. It does not, however, discuss the perils of the Social Security system.

One dissenter to the SAVER Act was Indiana Representative Mark Edward Souder (R), who said that people are not ignorant about the need to save, but rather are income stressed—another way of saying overtaxed. Souder believes that an honest discussion of Social Security will be beneficial to the public's interests. I agree. The SAVER Act is a step in the right direction, if for no other reason than it raises public awareness of the problem.

Americans understand the need to save for retirement, but suffer from a lack of discipline to do so. In polls such as the one previously discussed, respondents have been asked what type of savings program they prefer. Three-quarters of respondents said that they prefer automatic deductions from their paychecks for savings instead of having to make conscious saving decisions every week. This suggests that a mandatory retirement savings plan would be needed to replace the current system.

Social Security's goal is not the problem, but its application is a failure. Obviously, something must be done now before the situation truly does become a crisis. Under a mandatory retirement savings plan, some investors will place money in equities. Among those stocks are bound to be components of the Dow Jones Industrial Average, and such investing would spur the Dow, as well as the overall stock market.

PRIVATIZATION

There is a better way. The privatization of public pension programs has been used throughout the world in various forms and with varying degrees of success as a solution to the large financial burden that public pension programs place on governments.

Talk of privatization in the United States began when former Senator Alan Simpson (R) and Senator Bob Kerrey (D) introduced a plan where individuals would have access to 2 percent of their Social Security contributions (the approximate amount of the surplus) to invest for themselves. The Simpson-Kerrey bill never saw much action on Capitol Hill. The model of privatization began in 1981 by Chile, but models in Great Britain, Australia, and Singapore have also had a great deal of success. However, some privatization models have not met with great success.

The less successful private plans have maintained heavy government involvement in their management, often with the government directly investing contributions for individuals. Those plans are popular throughout Latin America, East Asia, and Africa. With the exceptions of Singapore and Malaysia, the public-private plans have failed to produce positive results.

Even in Singapore and Malaysia, the public-private plans have underperformed privately managed funds. Furthermore, a large block of public money invested in private firms creates a tenuous political situation. For example, in terms of application in the United States, what if the federal government invested pension funds in Microsoft? In light of the Justice Department's anti-trust lawsuit against Microsoft, some serious conflicts of interest might be created.

Privatization is a relative term. True reform calls for legislators to make bold and decisive changes. We have identified several reasons why Social Security privatization is necessary. The following points are critical to privatizing Social Security.

 • According to federal government actuaries, the Social Security trust will exhaust its assets in 2032. At that point, inflows will cover only 75 percent of benefit payments.

- Even if benefits can be paid, the average couple in the United States will receive a real rate of return of less than 1 percent. Higher-than-average income earners, those who earned more than $22,675 in 1998, will realize a negative or zero rate of return. Private management, conversely, earning a conservative 4 percent real (i.e., the difference between yield and inflation) rate of return will generate the average couple a nest egg of $1 million at retirement. This will provide a $44,000 per year income stream, leaving the $1 million base largely intact for heirs.

- The pay-as-you-go system depresses national savings, which in turn leads to increased interest rates, lowered productivity, and stunted economic growth. That creates a downward spiral of reduced corporate profits, increased unemployment, lowered earnings, and diminished consumer spending, all of which have an adverse effect on the stock market, including the Dow Jones Industrial Average.

- A private system offers an opportunity for some Americans to break the cycle of poverty by passing savings on to their heirs.

- Individuals may choose when they want to retire and know the amount they will receive.

One repeated criticism of privatization is that of assessing the amount of risk borne by individuals. They will have to absorb market risk and, theoretically may have to stop participating at an inopportune time when their benefits will not be as great as they could be. Criticism such as this ignores some simple facts. Most investors will have invested in the stock market for a significant amount of time. Over the long haul, the market has historically outperformed the return on Social Security payments by a significant difference. Even if individuals have to cash out on downturns in the market, it is more than likely that their cumulative returns will be superior to what they would have been under the current system.

Further, the government is not immune to market risk either. That is, when the economy turns down, the government also sees a significant drop in revenues.

The risk that current contributors are absorbing by making Social Security payments into a system that has no chance of ever paying them a fair return is far greater than any systematic and timing risk they may face in a private system.

If ever there was a time to privatize, it is now. Polls regularly show that an overwhelming majority of adults 30 or more years away from retirement favor a privatized Social Security system. Public opinion is definitely in favor of privatization.

METHODOLOGY

There are many proposals regarding Social Security reform that involve some form of privatization. One self-described privatization plan calls for the government to maintain control of the Social Security fund and directly invest its proceeds in private companies.

Some politicians and economists support the Maintenance of Benefit plan as a compromise between full-scale privatization and simply maintaining the status quo. They concede the problems associated with the poor return on investment under the current program, but their solution to the problem leads to an ineffectual middle ground. They stop short of completely returning Social Security taxes to individuals to make their own investment decisions.

Under the Maintenance of Benefit plan, the government would invest Social Security surpluses directly into private firms and organizations. In addition, the current trust fund, which is invested in government bonds, would be partially transferred into equities. On the surface, this appears to fix part of the problem with Social Security, that of poor return on investment. However, that plan makes several fallacious assumptions as well as opens up serious questions about possible socialization and politicization of the American economy.

The Maintenance of Benefit plan would involve the federal government's direct investment of the Social Security trust fund ($656 billion) in the stock market. This system is based on the belief that Americans do not possess the know-how to create a desirable retirement for themselves. Maintenance of Benefit programs assume that the government is better qualified than individuals to assess their own retirement needs. Aside from this philosophical difference, the plan could have disastrous effects. Under this system, the American stock market would become socialized.

Under a program such as this, the government would have a significant stake in the outcome of the market, and the likelihood that it would interfere in market movements to manipulate the results would increase, thus threatening market stability. Then there is the potential that investment decisions may be based on firms' socially desirable outcomes, whether or not they maximize their shareholders' wealth.

Former Labor Secretary Robert Reich has suggested that private retirement plans should earmark a certain portion of funds for economically targeted investments, which have collateral benefits, such as affordable housing, infrastructure improvements, and job creation. Private management firms, on the other hand, are legally and ethically required to maximize returns for shareholders.

More important, the Maintenance of Benefit plan assumes that the trust fund exists in real terms, which it does not. This is explained in more detail later. But first, let's suppose that this system is viable. Under the Maintenance of Benefit plan, even if the government does not exercise its shareholder rights, fund managers would own a concentrated block of securities that would be uniformly voted. Those managers then become answerable to no one, deriving all of their authority from the aggregated funds of Americans. Effectively, that system hands over a significant amount of power to unelected officials.

Government investing opens up a host of problems. What companies should receive investments? What companies should be avoided? Are companies to be chosen based on social issues, for example, avoiding cigarette companies? How about investing in companies with nonunion employees? How about Microsoft? The examples go on and on.

The ensuing political chaos could be destructive. The temptation for government to get involved in manipulating outcomes is impossible to regulate away. Even with initial claims to maintain a hands-off policy, it is hard to imagine that policy lasting very long.

Government investing would also lower market returns. The government might avoid investing in companies because of social concerns or legal actions involving a company or industry. If the government refuses to invest in one or more of the Dow components, it would adversely affect not only the companies out of favor, but also distort the Dow's performance. According to a World Bank study, government-managed pension funds underperform private pension funds.

Government investment in the stock market would hurt market efficiency, because passive investment allows managers to be less vigilant in their quest for profitability. As evidenced by the Soviet experience, managers of firms are often political appointees, rather than visionary leaders, and visionaries may have views opposing those of government officials.

The assumption is that the Social Security trust fund represents real assets. The fact is that the Social Security trust fund is nothing but a bag of IOUs. It contains government bonds, money the government owes itself. As is well known, the annual surpluses that many thought were being used to build up a reserve for baby boomers have been spent on other government programs. The reality is that the federal government cannot write IOUs to itself and have them represent real assets any more than someone can write himself or herself a promissory note and expect it to represent an asset. It's money that the government has already spent.

One of Washington's secrets is that the annual Social Security surplus is used to lower the deficit. The government's balanced budget plan relies on $450 billion in Social Security surpluses through 2002. In 1998, the federal deficit would have been $29 billion if the Social Security surplus were factored out. The true issue is one of fiscal control, something often talked about but rarely practiced in Washington. Thus, if the federal government wanted to invest the trust fund, it would have to call in payments for the bonds, payments from itself, which means it would have to raise taxes, cut benefits, or issue more debt, making a bad situation worse.

Obviously, a truly private system, such as the one in Chile, is superior to a government-run program. Private incentives are kept intact and control is maintained by individuals, not federal managers.

INDIVIDUAL RETIREMENT ACCOUNTS

The Chilean system of privately managed individual retirement accounts began in 1981. The Chilean government realized that it faced financial disaster if it did not act to solve the public pension program's large un-funded liability. Based on the ideas of Milton Friedman, the Chilean system allows individuals to choose between individual private accounts (similar to IRAs) or Social Security. Each company is then required to pay at least a minimum investment return, set as a percentage of the average return earned by all companies. Workers are free to switch investment companies, which fosters competition.

Retirement age is 65 for men, 60 for women. Workers may retire earlier once they accumulate sufficient funds to pay a minimum level of benefits, set as 50 percent of average earnings over the preceding 10 earning years. Workers can also speed up the process by contributing up to twice as much of the minimum 10 percent—tax free and indexed for inflation. Payroll taxes are completely abolished for those in the new private system.

Within 18 months of its introduction, 90 percent of Chilean workers opted for the private system. Although participants pay 40 percent less into the new system, benefits have increased up to 50 percent, effectively resulting in a tax cut. If a system similar to Chile's were enacted in the United States, it would pump some $100 billion of new money into the capital markets.

THE PRIVATE OPTION

I favor a variant of the Chilean system of retirement for the United States, and the highlights of that proposal are covered in this section.

Workers would choose a private investment account similar to an IRA, where workers and employers contribute 5 percent each. In 1999, the rate was 6.2 percent for Social Security. The difference of 1.2 percent each would be sent to the government to help pay for those on the existing plan where it is too late to switch. After all citizens are off the existing plan, 1.2 percent of the payroll tax is abolished. Workers would have the option to contribute a total of 20 percent of their incomes into the fund (15 percent worker, 5 percent employer).

Life and disability insurance.   A portion of benefits would be used to pay for life and disability insurance.

Investments.   Assets would be managed by professional investment firms. Those firms would apply for licenses to manage retirement accounts.

Taxation of the retirement accounts.   Contributions would be taxed, but returns would be tax-deferred until withdrawn, similar to an IRA.

Retirement benefits.   Benefits would be set by purchasing an annuity, or periodic withdrawals limited by government regulation, so that funds cannot be depleted too rapidly.

Minimum benefit.   Government would guarantee a minimum benefit. In Chile, government expenditures have been very low for this purpose. Private funds have done so well that there has been little need to subsidize benefits.

Right to stay in Social Security.   Workers would have the right to stay in the traditional system if they so desire. However, after the superiority of the new system has been demonstrated, it is likely a complete exodus from the old system would occur.

Social Security benefits.   There would be no reduction of benefits for current retirees. However, future retirees would be offered benefits within the scope of the financial resources that the government has available. That is, benefits would be indexed to inflation rather than increasing with workers' incomes. Retirement age would be raised two months per year, until it reaches 70 in the year 2030. Obviously, this would create a disincentive to stay in the old system.

The Proposed Plan's Advantages

The economic benefits of this plan include savings in time that employers waste in complying with government regulations, estimated to be in excess of $100 million per year. In addition, a slow and gradual phasing out of the employer portion of Social Security is estimated to save business $169.2 billion per year, injecting a boon into the economy. Job growth would benefit by reducing the tax penalty imposed on employment.

Analysts estimate that total annual income for an average family of four would increase by more than $5,000. Feldstein estimated that the value of those benefits to America by privatizing Social Security would reach an amazing $10–$20 trillion in today's dollars.

If there is any question whether this plan would work in the United States, one needs only to look at selected state and local government entities to find examples. One million state workers in California, Ohio, Nevada, Colorado, Maine, and the Texas counties of Galveston, Brazoria, and Matagorda enjoy the fruits of privatized Social Security. In the case of Texas, government employees chose to opt out of the public pension system in the 1980s. This occurred before Congress outlawed this option, probably because of the fear that the federal government would experience a mass exodus out of the Social Security plan.

The National Commission on Retirement Policy (NCRP) has proposed a more modest privatization plan. Highlights include:

- Raising the retirement age to 70 by 2029
- Eliminating the earnings test
- Cutting the payroll tax by two percentage points and earmarking those funds for individual savings accounts for persons under age 55

Though similar in nature to the more radical privatization plan presented earlier, the NCRP proposal appears to be more politically viable. While partially turning over the responsibility of preparing for retirement to individuals, the plan maintains the safety net attraction of the traditional system.

Financing the Transition

There are several models for financing the transition, the toughest task of privatization. Most include some form of explicit recognition of debt, combined with government spending cuts. I propose the following.

Replace Social Security benefits. As workers transfer to the new system, traditional benefits would be replaced by the new benefits. In the long run, the present system's benefits would be eliminated.

Reduce Social Security benefit growth. An inflation-indexed system would reduce the growth level of benefits.

Revenue feedback. New investment would spur economic growth and thus higher tax revenues for government.

Continue payroll tax. The 1.2 percent differential cited earlier would help fund the transition from the existing system to the new.

Social Security surpluses. Social Security surpluses diverted to other government programs would be outlawed. The current surpluses would help pay transition costs.

Sell government bonds. Friedman and James Buchanan, both Nobel Prize economists, have suggested this. The bonds would not involve new government debt, but simply recognize the debt that the government already owes because of Social Security, an unfunded liability.

Of course, that has an offsetting effect on the new savings generated, as the government will borrow these savings to pay for current obligations. Bond sales, however, when combined with minor spending cuts, would be only about $500 billion (in end-of-century dollars) over the first 12 years of the transition, representing a fraction of the new savings produced.

It would take about 10 years after the final issue to retire the new debt. Plus, the government would avoid the estimated $1 trillion in bond issues that it would need to finance the current system, beginning in 2012, as the system begins to run a deficit.

Sell government assets. Why not pay for the transition, which represents a one-time expense, with a one-time sale? The U.S. government could sell such assets as the Postal Service, electricity-generation facilities, and loan portfolios at an estimated total value of approximately $300 billion.

Cut other government spending. The federal government would need to cut spending by only 4 percent, or $60 billion, per year in concert with the other proposals for complete implementation, with no increase in outstanding debt.

Enhanced economic growth. The country would enjoy expanded economic growth, which would serve as a buffer for transition costs. It's entirely possible that the reforms may drive the economy to expand at a rate that covers the transition costs.

TAXES

The driving force in individual behavior is incentives. Social Security has created negative incentives because it penalizes those who save in favor of those who consume. Essentially, the government has stated its preference for consumption. Considering that the economy is, theoretically, driven by consumption, this comes as no surprise. However, the savings function should not be underestimated. Savings help keep interest rates down and spur investment. Innovations and technological advancements are created from those investments.

Taxes add another factor. Analysts are concerned about the after-tax returns, not just the pre-tax returns. When government taxes capital gains, interest income, or dividends, the government is creating a disincentive to save and invest. In the United States, the government taxes all of them. Corporate dividends are subject to double taxation. A company's profits are taxed at the corporate level, then taxed again in the form of dividends at the personal level.

Because capital gains are often cited as a tax on the rich, reducing the levy is thought to favor the wealthy. While the point is arguable, it is estimated that as much as two-thirds of a capital gains tax cut would benefit the top 1 percent of income earners. However, supporters of a capital gains tax reduction point out that taxes on capital gains end up hurting only the little guy because investment creates jobs and opportunities for all income earners. The economic effect is difficult to measure, but it seems reasonable.

Nevertheless, there are differences of opinion. Those on the political left generally decry any reduction in capital gains taxes, while those on the political right fight for it. The debate rages on. From a practical viewpoint, the capital gains tax cut would "cost" taxpayers and purportedly raise deficits. Supply-siders argue that the increase in growth in the economy would essentially nullify this effect, a theory difficult to test and even more difficult to prove.

I side with the argument that a tax on capital gains is anti-growth and, thus, hurts more people than it helps. Certain tax reductions, such as across-the-board cuts in income tax rates or cuts in the capital gains tax rate, stimulate the economy. A faster-growing economy not only strengthens tax receipts, recouping some of the revenue losses normally associated with tax cuts, but also produces more jobs and higher income.

Any time the federal government attempts to create a tax system in the name of fairness, it invariably hurts the little guy (such as the excise tax on yachts in the early 1990s). As Steve Forbes, publisher and a presidential candidate, once said, "We want to tax the fruit from the trees, not the trees themselves."

The possibility of further capital-gains tax cuts looks reasonable. Following his election in November 1998 as a Senator from New York State, I wrote to Charles Schumer, suggesting that he and his fellow Democrats strongly consider cutting the capital gains tax to 15 percent and eliminating inheritance taxes on farms and small businesses. I suggested that he look to the experience of former New York Governor Mario Cuomo and New York State revenues after the first capital gains tax cut was enacted. I also called attention to the effect that reduced hotel occupancy taxes had for New York

City Mayor Rudolph Giuliani in terms of increased revenues and a reinvigorated tourism industry. Finally, I added that, "As you probably know, today approximately 50 percent of the American people own stocks either directly or indirectly. By cutting the capital gains tax, you're not helping the so-called rich, but helping the American people save for the future and helping to increase the prosperity for our children and their children."

I believe that taxes are headed downward and that savings incentives, including a capital-gains tax reduction, are inevitable.

THE FEDERAL BUDGET DEFICIT

Any discussion on taxes must include a discussion about the federal deficit. Should it be a concern? Is it as big a problem as some analysts suggest? The budget deficit has disappeared, and federal government is enjoying budget surpluses. Much of the credit can be given to the stronger economy, which has helped increase tax receipts faster than what was projected. Ross Perot may also deserve some credit for bringing the issue to the forefront during his 1992 presidential campaign. As the public became aware of the possible dire consequences of the deficit, the issue received more and more attention from politicians and from the news media.

The public's insistence on government's fiscal responsibility forced Washington to take measurable strides toward balancing the budget. Finally, in 1997, Washington reached an agreement for a balanced budget by 2002, reaching its goal in 1998, thanks to a stronger than expected economy.

The subsequent 1998 budget deal was significant because it represents the dawn of a new era of Washington fiscal responsibility, or at least that is the hope.

Still, the question that leaves many economists shrugging their shoulders is: does the deficit really matter? And if so, does it matter for the reasons the general public is told?

Steven Landsburg, in *The Armchair Economist,* tackles this very subject along with Lauren J. Feinstone in the chapter, "The Mythology of Deficits." Landsburg argues convincingly that government deficits in and of themselves don't matter. To illustrate this concept, I've paraphrase Landsburg in the next paragraphs.

Suppose that you decide to buy $100 worth of clothes. Now you have three ways in which to pay the bill. Plan 1: pay $100 cash today. Plan 2: borrow $100 and pay in one year. Plan 3: borrow $100 and pay yearly interest payments in perpetuity. Suppose the interest rate is 10 percent.

With Plan 1, you withdraw $100. Therefore, you forego the $10 interest you would have earned over the next year and the total cost of the clothes is $110. With Plan 2, you pay $10 interest and $100 principal in one year, and the total cost of the clothes is $110. With Plan 3, you pay $10 interest in one year, but you must leave $100 in a bank account to cover the interest payments in perpetuity, thus the total cost of the clothes is $110.

Regardless of your financing decision, the cost remains the same. The real question is whether or not spending money on the clothes is the right thing to do in the first place. "Our primary concern should be with the level and composition of government spending, rather than with how that spending is financed."[4] And perhaps this is one of the attractions of a balanced budget: it forces discipline on free-spending politicians.

There is a natural tendency to associate balanced with good, but the two are not necessarily synonymous. Americans should be less concerned about how government is paying for its projects and more concerned about what those projects are and whether they are good investments.

To be completely fair regarding the methods of generating the deficit numbers, part or all of the unfunded liability for Social Security should be recognized. After all, these are liabilities on the federal government's balance sheet.

Peter Drucker suggests that government will need to go through a radical turnaround in order to accommodate the new economic environment. He cites three steps government must take in order to improve its function:

1. Abandonment of the things that do not work, the things that have never worked, the things that have outlived their usefulness and their capacity to contribute.

2. Concentrate on the things that do work, the things that produce results, the things that improve the organization's ability to perform.

3. Analyze the half-successes, the half-failures. A turnaround requires abandoning whatever does not perform and doing more of whatever does perform.

Drucker stresses that government must move beyond the nanny state if it is going to serve a useful purpose in the future. He points out that gov-

---

[4]Landsburg, *Armchair Economist*, p. 109.

ernment programs in and of themselves do not always fail, except when government itself runs the program. But when government outsources its programs, they tend to be much more successful,[5] which is precisely what I am suggesting with Social Security.

In the new information society, government, like individuals, must constantly change and reinvent itself in order to survive as a productive entity. Government will have to stop meddling in the social sphere and concentrate on making policy. Terminating useless projects and privatizing others would go a long way toward reducing the size and scope of government, reducing the deficit, and improving the productivity of those government projects that survive.

CONCLUSION

In this chapter, we have examined the state of the federal government's fiscal policy as of early 1999. I believe that there is a compelling reason for the government to privatize Social Security. The traditional Social Security system creates negative incentives in the economy, specifically on savings. The large unfunded liability that the United States is facing could very well cripple the federal government and send deficits soaring in the not-too-distant future.

With the impending retirement of the first wave of baby boomers, the demands placed on Social Security will only become worse. However, all is not lost. A properly structured private pension program, using the current payroll tax system, would not only be a great boon for future retirees, but also for the overall economy.

A long, drawn-out political dogfight involving the future of Social Security already has begun. I believe that the preponderance of evidence supports a privatization plan similar to that of Chile's. There is a swelling grassroots support for a functional, dynamic, private pension plan. This force will move the country closer to adopting a private plan with individual accounts, and the responsibility and incentives that go along with them.

It is unlikely, of course, that any of the reforms that I have suggested will be enacted tomorrow. In the early years of the twenty-first century, however, the federal government will be forced to look at, and very well may adopt, some form of privatization. It makes the most sense economi-

---

[5]Drucker, *Post-Capitalist Society*, p. 160.

cally and fiscally. If the stock market continues going higher without a major interruption, many Americans may have less need for Social Security because their investments will be able to fund their retirement years. The fact is that stocks go up because corporate profits go up. With a booming economy, low inflation, low interest rates, and high investment rates, corporate profits will surge. As corporate profits surge, so will the DJIA up to and beyond 40,000 by 2016.

4

Demographics and the "Post-Capitalist Society"

The world is experiencing unprecedented economic change. Gone are the failed communist regimes of Eastern Europe. Gone are many of the international trade barriers that have hindered economic growth in past years. The world is embarking on a new and exciting journey into an era when hard work will be rewarded, knowledge will be its primary resource, productivity will be imperative, and Western business practices will be embraced the world over.

The assortment of fundamental changes in the economic landscape has further added complexities to the already complex task of projecting economic trends. One trend in the United States is the fundamental shift in demographics, specifically the aging of the baby boom generation. In Asia, a new and restless MTV generation has been born, ready to take on the world. The structure of the global economy is changing from a labor- and capital-based economy to a knowledge-based economy.

What will be the implications of these changes on economic growth and, consequently, the Dow Jones Industrial Average? Is a period of economic prosperity on the way, greater than the world has ever seen? What effects will these shifts have on Corporate America? And what strategies will corporate America use to Capitalize on this opportunity?

THE BABY BOOMERS

Among those who believe that the economy is on the verge of unprecedented growth is economist Harry S. Dent, Jr. He foresees in his book, *The Great Boom Ahead,* that the American economy will experience an unparalleled surge because of the changing demographics of the United States, namely the baby boom generation's entrance into what he calls the "Spending Wave."

According to Dent, the strength of the economy depends on people's earning and spending patterns as they age and raise families. People between the ages of 45 and 50 are at their the peak spending years, which is confirmed by U.S. Department of Labor statistics that show that spending hits its peak at age 49.

The bulk of the baby boomers will reach age 49 on average between 2005 and 2009. Consequently, these baby boomers represent approximately 76 million consumers with unprecedented purchasing power. Consumer spending drives the economy. The baby boom generation represents approximately three-quarters of the workforce, thus earning most of the income.

According to the Spending Wave theory, consumers in their thirties and forties do the bulk of their spending on durable goods, as they raise their families, while concurrently attempting to move up the economic ladder. Individuals begin the spending cycle around age 25, as they marry, form households, and begin families. The point when the children of the household enter school has the larger effect especially as they enter their teens, complete high school, and prepare to go to college. Every parent knows the costs of raising children through the teenage years.

This period is followed by a saving and investing trend, as individuals save for retirement during their fifties and sixties. Although Dent discounts the effect the last activity plays, other economists believe this is an integral part. High levels of national savings lower interest rates and keep the cost of capital for businesses in ranges that increase profitability.

My outlook for emerging markets in Latin America, Europe, and Asia is that, as the middle class develops, demand for U.S. products and services will expand globally. This could help offset waning domestic demand, as a maturing population reduces its spending. In order to maximize the effect of the increased savings rates, government must shift its attitude by allowing people to keep more of what they earn, in order to save and invest.

A declining fiscal position will demand that government grow its way out of financial problems, which may be a result of Social Security's problems, as discussed in Chapter 3. Although fiscal conservatives have long suggested this remedy, it has only recently being proposed by mainstream politicians, who have witnessed its powerful effects.

This dynamic already is at work as the federal government, blessed by a strong economy, reached a balanced budget agreement without having to make any difficult spending decisions. In some ways, that is unfortunate, because lawmakers were spared being forced to control spending and reach a consensus about how to control the growth of entitlement spending.

The first wave of baby boomers is entering the saving stage, creating a large source of funds for investment, an integral component in the quest to keep interest rates low. Low interest rates are extremely important to supporting equity valuations. Historically, almost all major corrections in the stock market were preceded by high interest rates. As long as interest rates are low, there is reasonable justification for the valuations in the market.

With the prospect of Social Security privatization, another source of capital may become available, depending on the means of financing the program. If the federal government finances the transition with bonds, the resources freed up by the privatization will be exhausted. Thus, the effect on interest rates will be negligible. If the government finances the transition by privatizing some of its entities, its demand for resources should lessen. The resulting increased supply of funds available to the capital markets should help to lower interest rates.

Today, most baby boomers are in their thirties and forties, and evidence of their saving stage is readily apparent in the record levels of dollars being poured into mutual funds.

Around 2010, consumer spending will drive an expanding American economy characterized by low inflation, low interest rates, and high worker productivity. Clearly, the upswing in economic growth, combined with historically low inflation rates, supports this position. It should be noted that economic growth has largely been a supply-side phenomenon, driven by available capital. Looking at the historical evidence, there is a strong correlation between the habits of today's seniors as they relate to the generational wave theory and the economy. The relationship tracks the Standard & Poor's 500 Index so closely that it cannot be coincidence.

Another factor in the impending boom is the number of 25-year-olds. On average, at age 25, there is a strong increase in spending as people begin families, move into apartments, and purchase durable goods, such as their first cars. In fact, the 25-year-old demographic represents the

FIGURE 4-1

The Spending Wave: 44–46 Year Birth Lag

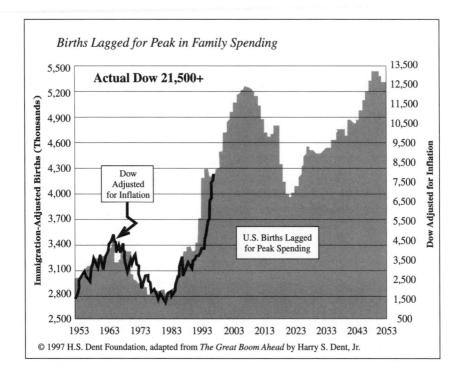

Births Lagged for Peak in Family Spending

© 1997 H.S. Dent Foundation, adapted from *The Great Boom Ahead* by Harry S. Dent, Jr.

largest percentage increase in spending. Figure 4-1 illustrates this phenomenon.[1] The next rise in 25-year-olds will begin in 2002, spurring on an already healthy economy.

Immigration provides further economic enhancement. According to Dent, the average immigrant to this country is about 30 years old, 15 years before the beginning of peak spending years. Therefore, there is likely to be a 15-year lag before new immigrants drive a major increase in spending and boost economic growth.

Using stock returns as a surrogate for economic growth, in the roughly 15 years after the 1843–54 immigration wave and the pre-World War I immigration wave, the market experienced significantly higher returns. The 1974–91 immigration wave would predict an effect on the

---

[1]Reprinted with the permission of Simon & Schuster, Inc. from *The Roaring 2000s* by Harry S. Dent, Jr. Copyright © 1998 by Harry Dent.

economy between 1990 and 2006. In fact, this immigration wave may well have contributed to the rise in stock values in the second half of the 1990s, particularly as immigration augments the baby boom effect.

Saving is a necessary component of a growing economy, and finances risk-taking and entrepreneurship. Because of the aging population, some industries, such as health care, financial services, and, most important, technology, will reap specific rewards.

ASIA'S YOUTH

As discussed in Chapter 2, global economic growth will present unprecedented opportunities for American firms. Part of this effect is captured in another major demographic event that has attracted attention, a shift in outlook among the youth of Asian countries.

Some economists believe this trend will have a greater impact on the economy than the aging and maturing of the baby boomers. The explanation for this shift is economic. While their parents grew up in hardship, Asian youths today are growing up in relative affluence and are adopting Western habits. They love our Coca-Cola, rock-'n'-roll, and blue jeans.

Further, as shown in Fig. 4-2, Asia's youth population is about 4 times greater than Africa's, 7 times the size of comparable groups in both

FIGURE 4-2

Huge Youth Market Emerging

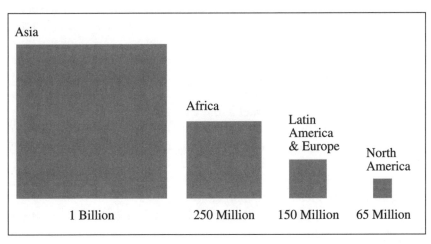

Latin America and Europe, and 16 times larger than in North America. With estimates exceeding 1 billion in total Asian population between the ages of 10 and 24, a major and dynamic market waits to be tapped.

Exporting Western culture has led some to believe that a high-growth market is available for some of the United States' mature firms. Indeed, companies such as Coca-Cola generate a larger share of their revenues from markets overseas. Those areas are among their highest-growth markets.

THE LONG-WAVE CYCLE

In the 1920s, Russian economist Nikolai Kondratieff developed his theory of the long-wave cycle. Kondratieff theorized that capitalist economies went through 48–60 year cycles with waves of renewal, growth, and correction. The important element of the theory is its relationship to the productive human life cycle. Demographics might also explain the long-wave theory. As baby boomers enter the growth stage of the cycle, expansion, high-capacity utilization, low unemployment, rising real wages, low real interest rates, rising debt, and optimism indicative of the growth stage follow.

When combined with the multitude of Third-World nations just beginning their capitalist era, as well as the changing culture in these nations, the world's largest-ever population is being incorporated into a long-wave capitalist economic cycle for the first time in history. And, it might be added, in a world with historically low levels of government interference. Will growth rates exceed even the highest expectations?

It is possible that several very powerful demographic events will occur simultaneously. The confluence of these trends causes many to speculate that the United States is about to experience an economic boom that could not possibly have been imagined. However, some concerns may need to be addressed, if and when markets are in the midst of such a surge.

Increased wealth stored in stocks may generate a large sell-off of shares, sending the market downward. Many economists believe that paper gains realized from a market boom do not have a large effect on consumption. Thus, there would be no impetus for a sell-off. I doubt that there is any major effect, however. After gains in the stock market in the early 1990s, personal consumption did not grow proportionately in the following years. It is reasonable to believe that baby boomers will keep their portfolios largely intact as the market goes up.

That is not to say conclusively that there will be no wealth effect and thus no corresponding increase in consumer demand and economic growth. If there is a wealth effect, it lags a few years as people wait to see how permanent the increase in wealth will be.

Nor does this suggest a sell-off at a later point. Rather, people will simply lower their rates of savings as their wealth increases. They will avoid paying taxes on capital gains as well as save on other transaction costs. I believe that if there is a wealth effect, it will not create any more volatility in the stock market than already seen. A lagging wealth effect is taking place, in fact, because increased consumer spending is outpacing increased consumer borrowing.

A POST-CAPITALIST SOCIETY

In the United States' post-capitalist society, the economic base is shifting from industrial to knowledge and service. Peter Drucker has studied the dynamics of this change and has delineated the challenges and problems associated with it. Drucker believes that the shift toward the post-capitalist society began with the G.I. Bill of Rights, created after World War II, for American military personnel returning to civilian life. This piece of legislation signaled the shift to a knowledge society by providing the means for thousands of veterans to further their educations.

Furthermore, this shift poses two primary challenges to the United States. First, the knowledge worker must consistently improve productivity. Second, the dignity of the service worker needs to be preserved. The service worker may lack the education to be a knowledge worker. Drucker writes, "And in every country, even the most highly advanced one, service workers will constitute the majority." This new era will be characterized by constant change, forcing all workers, knowledge and service, to "acquire new knowledge every four or five years, or else become obsolete."[2]

The key to success in the post-capitalist society is the ability to add knowledge to knowledge. The organization will become a key figure in this transformation. It will provide the tools for the individual to apply knowledge. Capital will serve the worker instead of the worker serving the capital. The organization's most important resource will be qualified, knowledgeable, and dedicated people.

The organization will also make knowledge productive by increasing specialization. Outsourcing will continue to be the wave of the future, offering opportunities for organizations that most efficiently perform

---

[2]Drucker, *Post-Capitalist Society*, p. 85.

given tasks. Outsourcing has become part of the American industrial landscape, not merely because of the economies involved. It also provides opportunities, jobs, and dignity for service workers.

The service worker, by definition, can see an improvement in wages only if productivity improves. Outsourcing provides that opportunity. It gives service workers the chance to earn income closer to that of knowledge workers.

Outsourcing will also help promote more equitable income distribution, because it results in higher productivity for both high-skilled and low-skilled work. Firms initially successful at providing value-added activities will have to continue to evolve and improve in order to survive. They must be constant innovators.

Perhaps most important, firms must be responsive. They will have to make decisions quickly. Decentralization will be the key to success in this new era. American firms have become adept at effecting positive change. Perhaps chiefly because of its flexible labor force, American firms have willingly taken sometimes-painful steps in order to answer the challenges that the changing structure of the economy poses. Now, American firms are lean and mean, and arguably the most proficient in the world at responding to change.

CONCLUSION

It is imperative that the federal government address its spending habits because today's strong revenue stream could decline should the economy slow down. Private retirement accounts must replace Social Security. The pay-as-you-go system will not be able to support future generations.

The shifting demographics of the United States are recognized as a dynamic economic force. If the theories in this chapter are correct, then all of us are about to witness an economic boom unlike any seen in recent history, and Dow 40,000 will be an inevitable part of this circumstance.

CHAPTER 5

Interest Rates
and Inflation

This brief chapter considers what inflation means to successful investing. In fact, interest rates may be the most important variable affecting the economy. Every great bear market is associated with high interest rates. Inherent in the calculation of interest rates is the inflation rate. Whether high interest rates are a cause of the bear market or a result of a bear market (or both) is open to speculation. In any event, if this great bull market is to continue, interest rates will certainly need to be low.

INTEREST RATES

Interest rates between 1991 and 1998 were relatively low and stable based on the yield of a 30-year U.S. Treasury bond. That yield averaged 6.7 percent, remaining within a 3.5 percent range from a high of 8.2 percent to a low of 4.7 percent. Although interest rates should be closer to 5.0 percent, investors felt a psychological barrier was preventing interest rates from falling below 6.0 percent. That is, until 1998, when interest rates began to tumble. At the end of the 1998, the 30-year Treasury was holding just above 5.0 percent.

It may help in understanding how interest rates affect the economy to think of interest rates as the price of consumption as opposed to the price of money. In other words, if the interest rate on a loan to buy a car is 10 percent, then the additional cost of buying a $20,000 car now instead of waiting a year is $2,000.

As interest rates decrease, the cost of buying becomes cheaper and, thus, the incentive to purchase immediately is increased. As interest rates rise, the cost to purchase increases and thus the incentive is to wait.

It is easy to understand why interest rates have such a powerful effect on the economy. Real interest rates (the difference between yield and inflation) are relatively high. While inflation may be near zero in the technologically led New Economy, real interest rates could be as high as 4 to 5 percent.

Nominal interest rates have remained relatively stable because of stable inflation, and it is entirely possible that interest rates will continue to decline. In fact, for the past 200 years, 90 percent of the time long-term interest rates have remained below 7 percent. Until the early 1990s, long-term interest rates had not been under 7 percent since the 1970s.

With inflation under control, some analysts felt that interest rates had remained artificially high because of the bond market's unwillingness to accept the concept of the New Economy. Low unemployment, high productivity, and modest inflation can live in harmony in an environment of consistent growth.

The trend toward the end of the twentieth century showed bond prices rising and yields falling, giving little reason to believe that the trend cannot continue. And with long-term interest rates falling below 5 percent in 1998, it appears that the bond market is beginning to accept the tenets of the New Economy. The stock market has adjusted more quickly than anticipated, and I am convinced that the stock market's impending boom, along with evidence supporting the New Economy idea, will force bond investors to change their approach to valuations.

With inflation held in check, it is reasonable to assume that interest rates will remain relatively low, or continue to trend downwards, for the foreseeable future. In fact, Salomon Smith Barney has observed that, in the past 200 years, there have been only 7 significant long-term changes in interest rate trends. Today, that seventh trend is under way. Each shift has lasted a minimum of 22 years, and an average of 30 years. The current downward trend is not yet 20 years old. If history is a guide, interest rates should continue in a downward trend, or remain steady, for at least 7 to 10 more years.

IS THE ECONOMY OVERHEATED?

I have continuously expressed optimism about the general direction of the economy and its positive effect on the Dow Jones Industrial Average.

History, however, has taught that good times cannot last forever. After all, the classic business cycle has both ups and downs. For this book, we are mostly concerned with the long-term general economic trends. Short-term corrections, however, could significantly divert attention from long-term goals. Following our previous consideration of interest rates and their importance, this section covers inflation and its effect on the economy.

The most formidable enemy of wealth creation is inflation, which must be taken into account in any analysis involving stock appreciation. On the surface, inflation will cause nominal stock values to increase. Consequently, there is no increase in real wealth, which is my principal concern. If the Dow goes to 40,000 by 2016 but inflation during that time is 10 percent, there will be very little increase in real wealth.

Inflation is really a modern phenomenon. Before 1933, prices fell in Britain and the United States in more years than they rose. Inflation was rarely a problem except during wars when government borrowing increased. The costs of inflation are often referred to as deadweight losses. Such losses can simply be defined as the costs that people and companies incur in order to avoid a loss, in this case inflation.

People carry less cash because cash loses value sitting in their pockets. This makes it more difficult to buy a sweater on a whim or to get through the day without a trip to the ATM. Retail stores keep less cash in the till and run out of change more often. Large firms keep less cash on hand to meet emergencies and have to meet those emergencies through borrowing, incurring additional costs. The deadweight losses because of inflation are estimated at $15 billion per year in the United States. These costs are accelerated in the case of hyperinflation, seen in the 1990s in Brazil and Russia. During the Weimar Republic days of post-World War I Germany, it was common practice for saloon customers to buy several mugs of beer at the beginning of the evening in case prices rose later in the evening. Warm beer was the cost of inflation.[1]

I do not expect inflation to be a significant problem during the Dow's rise to 40,000 because of the productivity phenomenon. Major productivity improvements have actually created an environment of disinflation. Instead of growth causing inflation, as is traditionally thought, growth has become disinflationary. I believe that prosperity is sustainable in the new productivity-led economy. Figure 5-1 illustrates the movement of the CPI since 1960.

---

[1]Landsburg, *Armchair Economist*, p. 68.

FIGURE 5-1

Consumer Price Index (CPI)

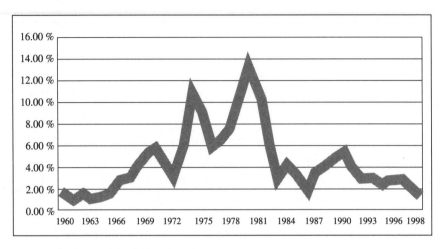

The quintessential models of economics suggest that after pro-longed waves of economic expansion, inflationary pressures eventually take over, interest rates rise, and economic growth slows. Inflationary pressures typically take two different forms: cost-push and demand-pull.

Cost-push inflationary pressure is associated with wage pressures. In tight labor markets, workers demand higher wages for the same amount of work. If a business cannot make up for the higher wages by means of productivity improvements, it will pass the costs on to consumers in the form of higher prices. The demand-pull inflationary pressure occurs when the demand for a good exceeds the supply by such a degree that a major price increase must take place in order for supply and demand to reach equilibrium. That is the case when too many dollars are chasing after too few products.

After these scenarios run their courses, a recession may occur, which could bring deflation. People save more, interest rates fall, pent-up demand is released, businesses restructure, and expansion takes place. Often a new technological advance initiates the expansion.

In 1998, U.S. unemployment fell to 4.6 percent and remained at or below 5 percent through the end of the year. That is below the historic 5.2–5.5 percent measure of unemployment, which is typically associated with cost-push inflation pressures. However, as pointed out, many analysts believe that we are in a New Economy where the typical economic models of the past no longer fully apply. The end of the Cold War and the high-tech revolution have released forces that are likely to boost economic growth and at the same time dampen inflation. The structure of global markets is becoming increasingly competitive. The high-technology revolution is boosting growth without putting upward pressure on prices.

STATISTICAL SHORTCOMINGS

In the New Economy, potential Gross Domestic Product (GDP) is understated because of inaccurate measures of productivity improvements. The technology revolution is constantly expanding the limits of the economy. Growth resulting from the high-technology revolution is, in fact, disinflationary.

Unemployment is falling chiefly because the jobs that are being created are in the professional and managerial labor sectors, which historically carry a near-zero unemployment rate. In fact, more than half of the job growth since 1987 has been in the professional and managerial sectors. Nationwide, unemployment is falling because the economy is creating more jobs in occupations with historically low unemployment rates. In addition, unemployment is dropping because older workers have lower unemployment rates than younger workers.

Labor statistics are a poor indicator for certain circumstances that are difficult to measure, understating the true labor condition in the United States. For example, people who have become discouraged in looking for jobs or have been unemployed for more than a year are not included in the unemployment statistics. Further, statistics don't count the underemployed, such as people with advanced degrees doing less than advanced work but hoping for an opportunity to go back into their chosen occupations.

Commodity prices have been stable or falling. The United States is in a non-inflationary environment, where the prices of goods and services remain relatively stable. Lower inflation supports lower bond yields and higher stock valuations.

Statistics show that computers accounted for one-third of GDP growth in the United States. Because computers and technology are falling in price, and the industry constitutes such a significant portion of GDP growth, worries concerning overheated growth are misplaced.

A key reason for this environment is the lack of inflationary pressures created by a bloated federal deficit. With the end of the Cold War and the world enjoying relative peace, the federal government can no longer use global uncertainty as a shield against criticism for its excessive spending. Thus, deficits have been shrinking. The falling American deficit should reduce both real and nominal interest rates.

In my view, government borrowing is the number-one influence on interest rates. Inflation can be suppressed temporarily because of international competition. Other countries are likely to counter any rise in prices in the United States by introducing goods and services to compete with domestic firms. That has been a major component in the Federal Reserve's decision not to raise interest rates to head off inflation. In an environment where international competitors enjoy advantages because of currency differentials, it would seem that American firms cannot raise prices, thus keeping inflation at bay.

There is some concern that low inflation cannot continue in light of healthy economic growth. With the unemployment rate dropping below 5 percent, there is concern that a tight labor market will lead to increased inflation. I believe that in the new global marketplace, where competition is constant and unceasing, American workers recognize the need for continued vigilance toward productivity.

Federal Reserve Chairman Alan Greenspan once stated that prosperity will reduce insecurity, and eventually workers will demand higher wages, resulting in inflationary pressures. I believe that everyone is working harder to beat the competition, and the competition is trying to do the same. In a competitive marketplace, no business is safe and no job is secure. Higher wages are a natural reflection of better jobs. Further, it should be noted that higher wages are not necessarily inflationary if they are accompanied by productivity improvements. When it comes to establishing monetary policy, of course, it's the Fed's opinion that counts, not mine.

CPI REVISIONS

Stanford University economist Michael Boskin chaired a commission that studied the Consumer Price Index (CPI), and in 1997, he announced recommendations for an improved index to measure inflation. In April 1998, the Federal Bureau of Labor Statistics announced modifications in the CPI, effective January 1999. Those changes reduce the increase in the index by about 0.8 percent annually.

Boskin estimated that the CPI, as formerly constituted, overstated inflation by 1.1 percent per year, with a substitution bias accounting for

0.5 percentage points. The substitution bias was the result of the CPI's inability to accommodate consumers changing from one product to another when the price of the first product rises over the second. For example, a rise in the price of butter might cause consumers to substitute less expensive margarine for butter.

Boskin said that the remaining 0.6 percent was a result of the CPI's inability to properly account for quality improvements and new goods. For example, automobile prices have gone up. However, if there are value-added items incorporated into a car, then the price rise is justifiable. The value of the product has increased and, therefore, the price rise is not simply a result of inflation.

For example, automobiles today perform at higher levels, they offer greater luxury and comfort, and they provide better fuel economy than in the past. The current CPI measure may not totally account for those quality improvements. Many analysts dispute the severity of the quality bias. Regardless, the study does highlight the need to create a more appropriate measure or to adjust the current standard.

Many measures used to gauge inflation may need to be re-evaluated. The Commodities Research Bureau index, which calculates the cost of raw materials, may no longer be an appropriate measure, because of the changing components of new technology. For example, silicon, a chief component of the semiconductor industry, is made from sand. Lasers use sand, light, and beryllium. Many of the raw materials needed for new technology processes are essentially free and, therefore, non-inflationary.

CONCLUSION

I cannot stress enough the importance of keeping interest rates and inflation low to push the bull market toward Dow 40,000. Every end to every great bull market in the history of the United States has been preceded by a major increase in interest rates.

It is hard to imagine a more conducive environment for investing than the one that has prevailed in the past several years. Further, low interest rates, low inflation, increasing corporate profits, expanding markets, relative world peace, and dynamic demographic shifts all point to this trend continuing.

If the leaders of the world continue to behave themselves, there is very little on the horizon that could end the greatest bull market the world has ever seen. And as I have demonstrated in this book, the best part is that it is only going to get better.

CHAPTER 6

Productivity and Technology

The fundamentals presented so far in Part 1 rely heavily on continued productivity improvements. It is the productivity of knowledge that is the determining factor in the competitive position of a company or an industry. Productivity, very simply, is applying knowledge to work. That is, finding and improving on the very best way to perform a given task. The world is in the middle of a shift to a society where knowledge is work.

The increasing number of entrepreneurial pursuits illustrates applying knowledge to knowledge. Organizing knowledge in palatable and in-demand forms will be the key to profiting from the information superhighway. For example, *The Value Line Investment Survey* is such a profitable and highly in-demand product not only because of the information it contains, but also because of the organization of that information. The knowledge is the data that Value Line possesses. The value added is the process that Value Line has undertaken to organize the data in readable and readily understandable formats. That makes things easy for users.

Data become information only when organized into a useful format. Consequently, this chapter looks at productivity and how it will affect the future growth of the Dow Jones Industrial Average (DJIA) and the general economy.

THE IMPORTANCE OF PRODUCTIVITY

The importance of productivity can be found in the numbers. If a nation's productivity grows at 1 percent per year, it takes around 70 years to double the nation's standard of living. If productivity grows at 3 percent per year, it takes about 23 years to double the standard of living. A nation that experiences 3 percent growth in productivity will be four times wealthier in 70 years than one that experiences only 1 percent growth. Productivity underlies all of the increases in both standard of living and quality of life in developed countries.

American workers are among the most productive in the world. Compensation costs of American workers average $17.28 per hour, compared to Japan's $23.66 per hour and Germany's $31.88 per hour. Hourly compensation in the United States is lower than that in 10 European countries. Obviously, this places American firms at the forefront in their ability to compete in this new global era.

It appears that the returns of being a productive nation are beginning to be recognized. A surge in American exports has placed the United States in what some are calling the golden age of exports. Today, American exports account for 10 percent of the Gross Domestic Product (GDP) compared to 7 percent toward the end of the 1980s. The value of U.S. exports exceeds that of any other G-8 nation.

Import numbers, however, are deceiving. Estimates have shown that roughly one-third of U.S. imports are from foreign branches of American companies, but they remain a part of import calculations. Factoring out these imports, as a percentage of the GDP, the deficit actually declined in the 10 years through 1998.

The productivity increases of the late 1990s are well documented. Economic recovery in the 1990s can be traced to productivity enhancements. Typically, productivity improvements account for approximately 54 percent of the overall GDP growth during an economic recovery. In the latest recovery and boom, productivity improvements accounted for an astounding 80 percent of GDP growth.

Many are concerned that these productivity gains were a one-time event brought on by massive corporate downsizing and restructuring. Such gains would seem to be one-time effects, unlikely to have long-term, sustainable effects on increasing productivity. The question becomes then: can Corporate America maintain these productivity improvements?

It is entirely possible to maintain and improve on early productivity gains. In the initial stages of recovery, most of which was gained through such steps as downsizing and layoffs, productivity becomes high. Next, there is an increased demand for technology to improve efficiency of labor and capital, which creates jobs and is characterized by increasing demand for highly skilled workers. In conjunction with the increased demand for technology, there must be continuous improvement in human capital. This calls for capital investments and increasing worker skills.

If the DJIA is going to reach 40,000, productivity will play a major role, and corporate America may have to face the issue of a potentially less prepared workforce. Further, the United States must address four other potential problems if it is to compete in a global market: a low savings rate, inadequate corporate investments in research and development, insufficient talent in the workforce, and low mathematics and science skills.

The solution to the education problem is not to pour more money into a broken system, but to use more efficiently the resources currently available in education. Many schools, predominantly universities, are proud of their decreasing student-faculty ratios. Yet if students are graduating increasingly ill-prepared for the workforce, schools have become less productive, because tuition increases have outpaced inflation. More money won't necessarily fix the problem. Americans must define the purpose of the school. It is not social improvement. It is teaching and learning. Schools must be held accountable for results, as are other organizations. Otherwise, the underperformance of American students on standardized tests compared with those in other advanced economies will continue.

The implications of this underperformance are far-reaching. Corporations may have to invest more heavily in training their employees to compensate for the inadequacy of the education system. In fact, throughout the 1990s, national human resource and training journals featured numerous reports on the costs of training employees, as well as putting forth innovative approaches. For example, a group of Fortune 500 companies joined forces in 1996 to reduce training costs while creating a more skilled workforce. Among the first to commit to the alliance were General Motors Corp., Motorola Inc., 3M Co., and John Deere & Co.

Government cannot fill all the country's needs for an educated population. Corporate training programs and access to interactive media, computer, and communications programs will help to resolve the problems. Such programs will supplement traditional educational resources. Clearly, firms are making conscious decisions to improve productivity, and this is not merely a random phenomenon. Corporate America's adoption of productivity enhancements is a necessary strategy for survival.

Productivity improvements have become popular because of global competition and slow economic growth. Increasingly price-sensitive consumers also make it more difficult to expand profitability through price boosts. A fiercely competitive global market is the key reason I believe that high growth, low inflation, and low interest rates can and will live in harmony. Competition is so intense that companies simply cannot raise their prices and expect to remain competitive. As a result, price inflation will remain near zero.

Profit margins are maintained in a weak pricing environment because companies are introducing new products and services at a faster rate. The message is clear: innovate or die. Or, to paraphrase an old saw, competition is the mother of invention. Not even large firms can escape the discipline of constant innovation. Microsoft, for example, has systematically chosen to acquire smaller innovative firms in order to expand its growth potential and to improve productivity.

The economic engine is driving the American economy toward disinflation, following generations accustomed to inflation. A multitude of factors is fueling this disinflation, including productivity gains resulting from the use of computers and networks, and global trade. Despite these gains, however, productivity improvements may be underestimated.

The movement in Washington to create a new index to gauge inflation gained momentum in January 1999. The revised CPI takes into account changes in consumer buying patterns. For example, instead of buying brand-name products, shoppers have become comfortable with the quality of generic products. Generic drugs routinely replace branded pharmaceuticals.

The CPI is also used as a measure to adjust government entitlement payments, such as Social Security and military pensions. Over long periods of time, such CPI overestimates as Boskin's 1.1 percent had a significant effect on all measures that use CPI as part of their formulas, including real GDP and productivity measures.

The Federal Reserve Bank of Philadelphia estimated that since 1975, the economy has grown twice as fast as previously measured and that productivity is three times as much. To explain lower per-unit labor costs, some analysts question whether the United States has developed a new model of manufacturing, perhaps one that is more efficient than any place in the world. The creation of a new system would imply that the productivity gains are permanent and may be sustainable.

Several factors are involved in comparing the financial results between domestic and foreign firms and, thereby, can be used to draw conclusions about their systems. Currency fluctuations are one such factor. After currency adjustments are made, American labor costs are below those of our competitors.

INSTANT MANUFACTURING

Other factors that must be considered in the economic numbers game include increased sales volumes, increased labor productivity, and corporate downsizing. Still, these factors do not completely explain the explosion in corporate profits. Because of the efficient use of capital, the United States is enjoying one of the most productive eras in its history.

One explanation of soaring U.S. corporate profits is attributed to a superior form of manufacturing called "instant manufacturing," or the ability of firms to create custom-made products and services for immediate delivery. For example, Dell Computer Corp. takes orders directly from customers via telephone and the Internet to produce computers configured to customers' specifications. Consequently, Dell has attained a higher degree of customer satisfaction and, potentially, repeat orders.

Consumers will soon be able to place orders for specific vehicle makes, models, and options via the Internet. The manufacturer will produce the vehicle to customer specifications and deliver it to the outlet nearest the buyer. The future of manufacturing lies in mass customization. Companies produce large quantities of smaller lots to higher specifications and quality standards in quick response to customer orders.

A report by the McKinsey Global Institute appears to support the conclusion that American firms are improving their capital productivity. The report notes that despite a much lower savings rate than Japan and Germany, the United States created $26,500 in new wealth per person between 1974 and 1993, while Germany created $21,900 and Japan $20,900. The report concludes that it is the United States' superior capital productivity that has led to American industry's return of capital, outpacing Germany's and Japan's return of capital: 9 percent for the United States and 7 percent each for Japan and Germany. The creativity in management, marketing, and financing practices exhibited by American executives outpaces their international competition.

Part of this superior capital productivity can be attributed to the increase in specialization among both manufacturing and service firms. Outsourcing, or contracting with another firm to handle a part of the manufacturing of a product or providing a service, is increasingly popular among U.S. firms. The reasoning behind this strategy is that the principal firm enjoys cost advantages by using the contracting firm. The latter can often perform the function previously performed by the principal firm more efficiently, thereby passing back the cost savings.

There is also a trend in Corporate America toward smaller, streamlined corporations that specialize in a particular service. The movement away from diversification and more toward specialization is partly a result of the economy's change from a manufacturing-based economy to a service-based economy. In a service company, economies of scale are not as necessary as they are in a manufacturing company. Even in manufacturing firms, however, outsourcing is an efficient way to take advantage of other firms' specialization.

Since the mid-1970s, Fortune 500 companies' employment rolls have dropped by more than one-fourth, from 16.2 million to 11.8 million. It is not necessary to look far to find examples of large firms slimming down payrolls. AT&T, IBM, Union Carbide Corporation, and Eastman Kodak Co. have all gone through highly publicized restructuring programs designed to streamline corporate operations. Meanwhile, smaller firms have picked up the slack in employment.

A type of regression to the mean is taking place in American business, where large firms are downsizing and small firms are upsizing, all of which makes perfect sense because the tasks being outsourced don't disappear; they still need to be done. Smaller firms that have chosen to specialize in performing these tasks have hired many of the displaced workers laid off by the larger firms. All of this suggests that productivity gains can be maintained and that future high growth rates in the equity markets are justifiable.

The new management style developed partly because of United States accounting practices, specifically, activity-based costing. This accounting method allows managers to more efficiently identify profit and cost centers, leading companies to cut waste and to outsource functions.

Gains in productivity are essential if American firms are to survive in the new global environment. One observation is that American firms were seeing poor returns on technology investments in the 1980s. American firms, particularly service firms, were investing billions of dollars in information technologies and receiving little or no return in terms of increased productivity.

Service firms in particular accounted for more than 80 percent of the investment in new technologies during the 1980s. Because service companies were essentially shielded from global forces, open-ended hiring and indiscriminate technology acquisition plagued the industry. Eighteen million workers were added to service payrolls in the 1980s, many of them performing low to no value-added functions. However, deregulation and the emergence of foreign competitors forced Corporate America to solve the technology quandary. It now appears that managers are tapping efficiencies long embedded in America's massive infrastructure of information technology.

As global competition increases, managers will be forced to seek productivity enhancements in order to maintain profit margins. They must find ways to link technology with efficiency gains in a weak pricing environment. As long as competitive pressures continue, this trend is likely to continue. One area where the trend is strong is in the computer industry, which many credit for leading the way in economic growth. According to the federal Bureau of Labor Statistics, at year-end 1998, for the first time, knowledge-based industries led all other sectors in job creation. The technology sector continues to advance even as prices fall and the power of technology improves exponentially.

Higher growth doesn't always mean higher prices. Because the high-tech industry is providing much of the growth in the economy, the concern for price inflation is unwarranted. Productivity gains will always bode well for companies' stock values, which suggests that a steadily growing DJIA is likely. Corporate bottom lines will grow at a faster rate as a result of productivity efficiencies, even in the absence of robust sales growth. Profits will grow because costs drop.

If competitive pressures remain high, Corporate America will be forced to seek productivity improvements to offset higher wage costs. Competitive pressures will not allow companies to pass on the costs to the consumer. Corporations will have to cut costs, hence bringing about greater productivity.

Along with corporate activity, government policy must provide incentives to corporations and individuals to become more productive. The trend in government toward a less demanding and less complex tax system will allow everyone to keep more of what is earned.

As long as technology advances, there is no reason to believe that the U.S. economy cannot continue to grow, perhaps at an even faster rate. Indeed, American industry is reaping improvements in productivity that, if continued, could sustain the current economic scenario into the foreseeable future.

TECHNOLOGY

The technology factor is the key force in the New Economy. Our projections assume a significant technology risk. That is, our forecasts are largely dependent upon technology continuing its rapid increase in implementation and its rapid fall in price. Technology is the key to growth in many segments of the New Economy. Investment in new technologies is the driving force behind growth. New technologies lead to more formidable competition and higher standards of living.

Advances in technology will affect all industries, not merely the classical technology industries. The printing industry, for example, has eliminated myriad steps in the book production process. Type is no longer set in hot lead; computers now not only compose type, they are also used in arranging text, design, and layout, sending the material directly to the press for printing.

Technology probably adds at least a full percentage point to the potential growth of the real economy, which suggests that the economy can grow at a faster pace than is traditionally accepted before inflation worries become relevant. Improved productivity generates improved profitability. As costs to Corporate America have decreased, firms have taken the cash and invested it back into the business, not only adding to payrolls but also heightening product quality. This characteristic of the New Economy leads economists to believe that Federal Reserve action is unnecessary, because disinflation is more relevant than inflation at current growth rates.

Today, we have seen only the tip of the technology iceberg. For example, most people do not yet have a computer and an Internet connection in their homes, so the direct producer-consumer connection has not yet been established on a wide-scale basis. However, the introductions of net computers, which use simpler computer chips to provide access to the Internet at more reasonable prices, may change this. When the direct producer-customer link does occur, cost savings will be generated as well as productivity improvements.

Compared to the rest of the world, the United States has a much more technologically educated workforce. The country enjoys the only technology surplus in the world. There is no equivalent to Silicon Valley in any other part of the globe. The United States' return to the top tier of manufacturing heralds a renaissance in the production of goods.

By the mid-1980s, computer memory chips had become a low-profit commodity. Intel made the difficult decision to lay off 30 percent of its workforce, while shifting from producing a low-end memory chip to the more advanced central processing unit chips. Subsequently, Intel has become the standard bearer among microprocessor producers and a top stock pick for droves of investors.

The United States leads the semiconductor business in almost every way: overall dollar volume, market share, profit margins, and product mix. Americans' acceptance of technology, and the rapid change it brings, suggests that the country will reap the benefits of productivity improvements and a higher national quality of life. Improved living standards have become ingrained in the American way of life as an ongoing process. More than a one-time event, improvements in the American standard of living will only continue to grow.

The technology advantage that American firms enjoy is significant not only for leading-edge industries, but also for older, more traditional industries, such as steel manufacturing. Because of the productivity improvements brought about by technology advances, domestic steel is cheaper than foreign steel, absent transportation costs. In fact, domestic steel producers can no longer meet American demand. Nucor Corporation highlights the trend of traditional industry going high-tech. Based in Charlotte, North Carolina, Nucor took advantage of new advanced technology ovens, allowing it to be profitable and still underprice foreign producers.

A portion of the technology benefit traces to the end of the Cold War. When military technology was declassified, entrepreneurs quickly found new uses for valuable research that had been hidden in top-secret government labs. In addition, some of America's best and brightest scientists and technicians were previously involved in creating technologies for military purposes. Those talents are now creating products and services for general consumption. In fact, the end of the Cold War may be the most bullish event of all time. It may even be compared to the opening of the American frontier during the second half of the 1800s in terms of creating a new era of economic opportunities.

THE INTERNET AGE

Communication has become synonymous with the economy. As new technology speeds the transmission of knowledge, the unrelenting drive of incremental growth also speeds up. Manufacturing is no longer the backbone of the American economy; information has taken its place. Productivity soon may no longer be the benchmark to measure the progress of the U.S. economy. The pace of ideas and innovations generated by American industries may become the more accurate measure to evaluate progress.

The New Economy is fueled by communication and information, and the Internet is the place to be as the world embarks on its journey into the twenty-first century. Going online is the latest, fastest, and soon-to-be universal way of obtaining information. Moreover, the information available on the Internet has become, and will continue to be, the catalyst for increases in productivity, wealth, and convenience in Americans' lives.

Mastering the use of computers and the Internet may seem a daunting task to some, but those skills are becoming vital to everyday life. It will be incumbent upon Americans to become familiar with this technological advance and to embrace its significance as a catalyst for a flourishing global economy. The online economy is estimated to reach $1 trillion in 2000. The distinctions between the network economy and the industrial economy will blur and fade as a result of the relentless advance of online commerce. The Internet is growing at a record pace. During the first 1,000 days of the World Wide Web's life, 450,000 websites and thousands of virtual communities were created, essentially for free. Never before had an emerging medium experienced such rapid acceptance so early in its life.

Some telephony experts foresee the time when data traffic on global phone lines will overtake voice traffic. In the late 1990s, voice traffic volume was 1,000 times that of data traffic, but that ratio is expected to flip by 2001. More machines will be talking to machines than humans talking to humans. In fact, according to Lucent Technologies, data traffic could be 10 times voice traffic by 2005.

While most industries were cutting jobs by one-fifth during the 1990s, the technology sector was creating jobs and seeking qualified people to fill them. Between 1994 and 1998 alone, the technology industry added 10 million jobs in the United States. Louise Yamada, senior technical analyst/vice president for research at Salomon Smith Barney, asserts that technology represents about one-third of United States economic growth, creating a $3 billion trade surplus in knowledge-related services.

The emergence of the Internet in the 1990s as a dominating element in American life can be compared to the introduction of the automobile. Although invented in the mid-1880s, automobiles did not begin to reach the buying public until the first decade of the 1900s. Automobiles were first viewed as luxury items for the wealthy. By 1928, however, cars had a market penetration of 50 percent. By 1942, cars were considered a necessity among the middle class.

Just as the spread of the automobile sparked the American economy after the Great Depression, the Internet is fomenting another economic revolution, the network revolution. In 1996, personal computers achieved a 40 percent market penetration in American homes, with the Internet as the force driving the network revolution into the mainstream at the end of the millennium. Ninety percent of urban and suburban households are projected to access the Internet by 2010.

Federal Reserve Chairman Alan Greenspan foresaw the impact of Internet stocks on the stock market and the economy as ranking with the steam engine, steel, electricity, and semiconductors as a seminal technological development. He cited high-tech companies Amazon.com Inc. and Yahoo! Inc. as two heavy hitters in the industry (and in the market).

The emerging dominance of the Internet and the information revolution will change just about everything in people's daily lives. The computer-driven information revolution will not only change the way people communicate, but also will alter the way they live, work, and think. The Internet has created unprecedented convenience for doing business, and more information is accessible more quickly and easily than ever before in history, all of which can be shared with others at the click of a mouse.

INTERNET SHOPPING

Information, however, is not the only commodity available on the Internet. There are hundreds of places to shop and thousands of products offered for sale online. For some online merchants, December 25 is more than a white Christmas, it's a web Christmas.

Consider that, in 1998, holiday shopping alone was estimated at $2.3 billion for Internet stores. Although this may represent only a small percentage of overall U.S. holiday spending, it is well more than double the previous year's total. Merchants who miss a Christmas season online are one more year behind when the next Christmas comes, and most retail experts agree that a failure to reach out to customers online can result in a merchant going the way of Woolworth. Missing online customers leaves merchants at serious financial risk.

Although the holidays may be the most popular time to shop, an estimated 17 million people made purchases from a website in 1998. Those numbers are rising every year. In 1997, 10 million people shopped online, double the number of shoppers the prior year. The most obvious benefit of cyber shopping is significant time savings. It's not necessary to drive to the mall, search for a parking space, and then navigate through the crowds, only to stand in a long line waiting to pay. Instead, shoppers log onto the Internet, navigate to the website where they want to shop, load up a cyberspace shopping cart with mouse clicks, transmit credit card data, and wait for the package to be delivered. Shopping online is simply easier, less stressful, and less time-consuming than traditional retail shopping.

Nevertheless, cyber shopping today can still be troublesome and lengthy. If conflicts arise or there are questions concerning a product, most sites do not offer instant feedback or answers. There is no human to respond to questions or to direct shoppers to their objectives. Waiting usually involves downloading information from a website. Depending upon computer and hard drive capabilities, modem speed, and connection, this can be time-consuming. Still, long waits and shopping frustrations may be easier to handle online than standing in line behind a dozen other shoppers or trying to find a parking spot.

While there are glitches in cyber shopping, solutions are being introduced to resolve the problems. As the process improves, shopping online may replace many tedious errands in everyday life. Shopping in the Internet Age will mean exchanging time now spent on some monotonous tasks for pursuing enjoyable activities.

Tennis, anyone?

E-MAIL COMMUNICATION

E-mail, or electronic mail, is another key feature of the Internet that is drastically changing how we communicate in everyday life. It has been estimated that more than 2 billion e-mail messages were sent daily in 1998 in the United States, almost double the volume sent in 1997. And the number of daily messages is expected to climb to 8 billion by 2002.

E-mail has been in use since the 1960s but underwent significant changes in the 1970s when machine-to-machine e-mail was introduced. Traffic has not stopped growing since. E-mail offers a fast, easy, and inexpensive way to communicate with family, friends, and business associates.

In the business world, e-mail allows coworkers to send information in seconds, regardless of location. As the ranks of top executives fill with the Internet-savvy, and the traditional office becomes increasingly non-site specific, top-level decisions may be made by managers in sweat suits instead of business suits. Meetings will convene in cyberspace instead of the conference room, since it will no longer be necessary to fight traffic jams to attend business sessions. In fact, working from home or in small satellite offices is the wave of the future. Telecommuting to a job instead of driving to work will become increasingly popular in the coming years.

The Internet embodies the time-honored American ideal of equality. Employees can communicate from any location via the Internet, irrespective of the size of their companies. They can exchange ideas, participate in decision-making processes, and distribute information in a timely and efficient way.

Information and its ally, the Internet, will continue to change the way people communicate for decades to come. People will storm the dataways in search of information and diversion. They will learn and enjoy in ways beyond their imaginations. The Internet will turn ordinary people into extraordinary explorers. It will become, metaphorically, Christopher Columbus's flagship or Neil Armstrong's lunar lander.

PRODUCTIVITY AND THE BABY BOOMERS

Productivity gains are inevitable, thanks to the life cycles and influence of the baby boom generation. Young workers first entering the workforce tend to require a heavy training investment. As they mature in their occupations and become more productive, they require less investment from their firms. Ultimately, firms reap the rewards of their earlier investment.

The inflation increases that the United States suffered in the 1970s were, in large part, a result of this initial investment in the thousands of baby boomers entering the workforce. The productivity slowdown of the 1970s and 1980s was caused by earlier demographic shifts of workers from farms to factories, women entering the workforce, and the opening of the borders to immigrants in 1965.

These demographic shifts, along with the first wave of baby-boomer college graduates, increased the entry-level ranks of the American workforce. As baby boomers entered their thirties and forties, however, they became more productive and required little or no further investment. At age 40, workers are knowledgeable, seasoned, and responsible. They also are still young enough to be comparatively healthy.

It is estimated that baby boomers represent approximately 75 percent of the United States workforce. A high volume of extremely productive workers, combined with the lower total real investment needed for new employees and major capital and technological improvements, results in a high dividend paid on Corporate America's previous investments in training and development.

PRODUCTIVITY AND MEASUREMENT

A question that plagues productivity analysis is measurement. A curious gap in productivity growth has emerged between the manufacturing and total business segments. While manufacturing productivity improvement is measured at 4 percent, total business productivity is up only 0.5 percent, implying that productivity in the service sector has been declining. That does not seem possible with profits soaring in major service sectors.

The airline industry's return to profitability and service companies' continued investments in information systems, for example, suggest that there must be an increase in productivity not showing up in traditional measuring systems. That theory is seemingly confirmed by virtue of the gap between the Gross Domestic Product (GDP) and the Gross Domestic Income (GDI). In theory, these two numbers should be equal. In 1995 and 1996, GDI grew faster than GDP. In 1996, there was a gap of $75.1 billion between the two measures.

Because the GDI is greater than the GDP, economic growth has been higher than originally thought and American workers have been more productive than originally thought. Taking the sales per employee ratio as a proxy for productivity, a high degree of correlation exists between productivity and sales per employee.

Using sales per employee ratios as a measure of productivity, real sales per employee in service sectors are up 80 percent since 1977. This compares favorably to nonfarm and nonfinancial corporate sectors. Using the same measures, the nonfarm and nonfinancial corporate sectors' productivity is up only 18 percent and 29 percent, respectively, during the same time frame.

Since 1986, the highest gains have been in sectors where unit output is most difficult to measure: technology, communications, and health care. Yet, productivity gains reflect a broad trend, with every major sector registering improvement. In addition, corporate profits are soaring in a weak pricing environment. Clearly, there must be marked improvements in productivity that have not shown up in traditional measures.

Per capita income purchasing power is growing at a faster rate than traditional productivity measures since the mid-1980s, deviating from its normal high degree of correlation between the two measures. Productivity has been growing at least 3 percent annually since 1987.

Proof of productivity improvements in service industries is best exemplified by the decrease of inflation in service prices, which are a component of the former CPI, comprising 57 percent of the measure's makeup. Analysts credit improvements in productivity, along with increased competition and decreased regulation, to lower costs. Cost-control measures in the health-care industry, as well as lower housing costs, have helped suppress service inflation. On the manufacturing side, similar results can also be observed. Figure 6-1 shows that manufacturing wage increases have diminished.

One concern about the current values of stocks is relatively high price-to-earnings (P/E) ratios. As of early 1999, the 30 DJIA stocks

FIGURE 6-1

Wage Inflation Is Subdued

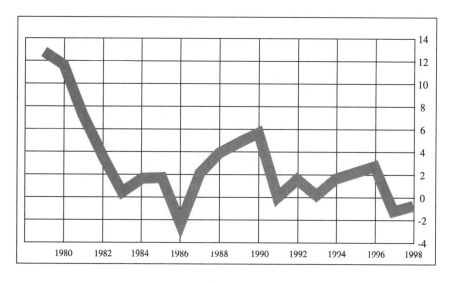

traded at an average 24 times earnings on a trailing basis and at a projected 20 times earnings for the future. Higher true profitability is usually associated with higher P/E ratios. Assuming that productivity improvements are synonymous with true profitability, perhaps the marketplace's higher P/E ratios are a reaction to the productivity boom. The low levels of inflation of the mid- to late 1990s affected stock valuations among investors seeking returns greater than those offered by fixed-income instruments. The alternative was stocks, and as demand for equities rose, P/E ratios rose in step.

Keep in mind that productivity improvements may be further underestimated because of the overestimated inflation number of the Consumer Price Index. Such a sustained increase could not continue if the economic news over that stretch was as dismal as the official figures indicate.

A common criticism on this outlook of strict productivity gains is the social cost. Continuous change, sudden downsizing, and related events lead to high employee displacements and accompanying dislocations. Employees often are caught poorly prepared for the troughs of the business cycle. The models advanced in this book speculate that the social cost can be a one-time event, which, in the case of the United States, was paid in the early 1990s.

Global competition will probably force managers to continuously seek out productivity enhancements. It will increase real wealth in wealthy economies through improved terms of trade, competition, economies of scale, and financial diversification. With improved terms of trade, American consumers will enjoy cheaper manufactured goods, such as clothing, because of the lower-cost labor used to produce them overseas. This will cause a real wealth increase in the United States. Through the 1990s, real prices fell 20 percent on those items.

In wealthy economies, there will almost certainly be an initial displacement of workers who produce these products. These workers can be retrained in areas where the United States has a greater competitive advantage, probably in higher-paying technical positions and professional-caliber service jobs. Americans' great propensity to accept change and answer challenges means that Americans will again rise to the occasion and answer the call to adapt to the changing economic environment.

Competition will probably be the biggest factor most affecting productivity. Staying ahead of Third-World producers might also encourage increased investment in human capital, further speeding growth. The economies of scale should increase as firms benefit from international markets, spreading fixed costs more widely. Innovation rewards will be higher, which also should speed technology. Finally, economic advances in Third-World countries will bring greater political stability, thereby lowering political risk and increasing efficient distribution of capital.

CONCLUSION

This book celebrates the United States' return to economic prominence, defying the naysayers who insist that the nation's best days are behind it. The United States has shown that, when it comes to change and responding to it, Americans are still number one. I believe that the United States' best days are ahead. While all is not perfect, the crucial indicators are very good. The nation enjoys perhaps the strongest economy in history.

The underlying economic fundamentals are about as sound as they can possibly be. Low interest rates, low inflation, and shrinking government, combined with the unique changes of the global expansion, shifting demographics, and relative world peace, make me feel very optimistic about the United States' future.

According to famed French novelist Anatole France, "The future is hidden even from those who make it." We cannot possibly forecast inevitable changes caused by innovation, wars, acts of God, and other unforeseen variables. No matter, at our investment advisory firm, we make reasonable assumptions every day about future events based on solid fundamental analysis, and we see Dow 40,000 by 2016.

TWO

WINNING INVESTMENT STRATEGIES FOR DOW 40,000

7

Winning Investment Strategies

P_{art} 2 of *Dow 40,000* contains practical, timely information, much of which can be used as a workbook for creating wealth. I foresee continued strength in the American stock market through the second decade of the twenty-first century. In order to take advantage of this forecast, our investment team has conducted an analysis of the industry sectors that we believe will lead the charge.

Although this book focuses on the Dow's prospects, we have selected the S&P 500 Composite Stock Price Index as the basis of our analysis. The S&P 500 is a broader measure of the market than the Dow Jones Industrial Average (DJIA) and contains distinct industry sectors.

The index consists of ten major sectors, as shown in Table 7-1, into which all common stocks in the S&P 500 are organized. These sectors are in turn subdivided into more specific industry groups. For our purposes, we confined the focus to the 10 major sectors in developing a portfolio structure.

DEVELOPING THEMES FOR EQUITY INVESTMENTS

Benjamin King, in his doctoral dissertation at the University of Chicago, published in 1964, showed in the period he studied (1952–60) that, on av-

TABLE 7-1

S&P 500 Major Industry Sectors

S&P Industry Sector	Weighting 12/31/98
Capital Goods-Technology	23.8%
Financial	15.5
Health Care	12.1
Consumer Cyclical	12.9
Consumer Staple	11.1
Utilities	7.7
Energy	6.2
Capital Goods-Industrial	6.5
Basic Industries	3.2
Transportation	0.9
	99.9%

erage, price changes in stocks could be attributed to four factors in the following percentages: market as a whole, 31 percent; basic industry, 12 percent; industry subgroup (or other common factors), 37 percent; and the specific company, 20 percent. More than three decades later, the results of King's research have not changed.[1]

Although the DJIA does not reflect the full range of industry sectors covering the majority of American common stocks, there are stocks in the S&P 500 that exhibit characteristics of those in the Dow 30. They are industry pacesetters, led by seasoned and solid management, and their stocks typically are in the large capitalization category. These Dow-like stocks generally have been in the market for a long time and are recognized leaders within their own industries or are at the fountainhead of their industry. Such stocks as Microsoft and Intel qualify as Dow-like stocks, even though they have been in the market for only about a quarter century. For technology stocks, however, that represents longevity.

For investment purposes, we use the S&P 500 as a tool in developing ideas concerning investment allocations to the sectors we believe will outperform in the coming 20 years. This leads to recommendations for individual investors to position their own portfolios. We have identified the following 10 sectors, or themes, for investment purposes:

---

[1]Hagin, Robert, with Mader, Chris. 1973. *Dow Jones-Irwin Guide to Common Stocks.* Homewood, Ill.: Dow Jones-Irwin, Inc., pp. 69–70.

1. **The capital goods-technology sector** represents the durable goods produced and consumed within the technology industries, including computer manufacturers, software producers, silicon chip fabricators, and communications networking equipment firms. Durable goods are generally defined as products that will remain in operation for three to five years at the least. The capital goods-technology group also includes aerospace and electronics manufacturers.

2. **The financial sector** encompasses banking, insurance, investment, and loan businesses that are responsible for monitoring, safekeeping, and distributing the financial assets that an aging population is accumulating to provide for their post-retirement years.

3. **Pharmaceuticals are the largest component of the health-care sector**, which also includes medical equipment and hospital management.

4. **Autos and retail make up the bulk of the consumer cyclicals sector,** a group that tends to be influenced by swings in consumer confidence. If consumers feel good about their jobs and future incomes, they are more likely to go shopping for new clothes or buy new cars sooner than if they were concerned about being laid off from their jobs.

5. **The consumer staples sector** includes those goods that are purchased regardless of economic conditions or consumer confidence. People will buy food, beverages, and household products regardless of their financial situation.

6. **Electric, natural gas, and telephone utilities make up the utilities sector.** These companies deliver the modern necessities of life to homes every day.

7. **The energy sector** includes oil and gas producers, drillers, and distributors. The largest component of this sector is the large multinational, vertically integrated oil companies.

8. **The capital goods-industrial sector** represents one element of the popularly called smokestack industries. Included are manufacturers of industrial products, such as machine tools and parts.

9. **The basic industries sector** provides the raw materials to manufacturers and consumers. Steel, aluminum, chemicals, and paper are the primary outputs from this sector.

10. **The transportation sector,** which touches American lives seemingly on a daily basis, is from the stock market's perspective, the smallest component of the marketplace. Airlines and rail provide the basis for this group.

We have selected three market-leading sectors on which to concentrate investments based largely on the patterns explored in Chapter 4 on demographics and the post-capitalist society. The aging American population, specifically the 76 million members of the baby boom generation, will more than likely focus a disproportionate amount of their money on three main groups: technology, health care, and financial services.

Consequently, these are the sectors where we recommend allocating most of the dollars within an investment portfolio. A broadly diversified portfolio, however, will most likely touch most of the S&P sectors in one way or another. The three sectors where we place a major portion of our investments tie in with the themes developed in the course of this book.

TECHNOLOGY

The technology sector is permeating all of the other sectors of the market, crossing industry lines. The momentum that has been generated in the years leading to the end of the twentieth century is going to explode in the twenty-first century. New technology will allow corporate America to continue to flourish, despite the loss of the experienced workers who will be retiring over the next 20 or more years.

In a world where corporate borders often do not coincide with international borders, technology not only allows managers to function on a global scale, but also allows for savvy users to maximize their global resources to boost profits.

Take, for example, an electric motors manufacturer operating in 10 countries worldwide. A manager at the United States plant needs coils to complete the production assignment for the quarter. Traditionally, the manager would have to contact all suppliers to see whether any could provide the product on short notice and, more than likely, at higher cost. As a result of technological advances, however, the manager first consults the companywide intranet resource to check inventory levels in the company's other plants and finds that the Malaysian plant has more than enough coils to complete the assignment.

As a result of the technology available from the desktop, the parts are shipped from Malaysia to the United States plant. Production is never interrupted, and by acquiring product from an Asian source, costs are reduced because of the relatively weak Malaysian currency versus the U.S. dollar. The manager is able to use parts that are already part of the company's assets. Thanks to technology available out of the box, profits will benefit.

Software allows suppliers to access their customers' databases over the Internet, so that they can more efficiently produce and deliver goods. As more businesses do so, productivity and profitability will be enhanced, which smooths out the traditional peaks and valleys of the economic cycle. With the proliferation of computers, networks, and the Internet, combined with the increasing convergence of voice and data communications, technology will continue to influence and dictate how business is conducted.

Any industry that is not taking advantage of technology is going to be left behind in what has become the vanguard of the Information Age. Companies need to automate routine and repetitive tasks, using computers and software to improve productivity in order to remain competitive in their markets. Technology already is playing a vital role in productivity improvements. Decision-makers are realizing that it is inefficient to saddle employees with routine and mundane tasks that a computer can do better. Technology can free those employees to devote their time and energy to much more value-added tasks.

At an elemental level, computers enable people to transmit information quickly and efficiently. Instead of dictating or handwriting a letter, having it transcribed and typed, then checking it, the writer simply enters it into the computer and, once satisfied with it, presses a key to transmit it to the recipient. Not only does this save time, it saves on personnel costs. The computer also can check math, spelling, and grammar, thus helping a user to avoid easily made mistakes.

Corporate investments in technology speed virtually every process in business while reducing or eliminating errors. This contributes to improved productivity and, ultimately, to increased profitability in the private sector. In the public sector, it can contribute to better services at lower taxpayer cost.

Technology is increasingly pervasive and is a major contributor to the ongoing growth potential that we see for another of our major themes: health care. Technology contributes to reducing the length of time and the expense of testing compounds for approval from the federal Food and Drug Administration (FDA). Pharmaceutical companies can develop computer models to determine how a compound will affect a patient, as well as interactions with other compounds.

By conducting experiments in cyberspace rather than with patients, pharmaceutical companies are able to determine more quickly and at a lower cost whether a compound should be researched and tested further or simply discarded. Thus, technology has become a critical research tool for pharmaceutical companies in developing, producing, seeking approval, and marketing new products.

Schering-Plough Corporation is only one pharmaceutical company that has used technology to speed the development of new drugs. Its research productivity has been greatly accelerated through new technologies in compound screening and drug testing. The company has increased the number of drug compounds tested annually from around 20,000 in 1992 to almost 900,000 compounds in 1997, a trend the company expects to continue.

New technology also permits researchers to move high volumes and high numbers of experimental compounds through the research and development system. In seeking a solution to a disease or disorder, the search field can be narrowed from thousands of prospects to a manageable number of compounds.

The technological breakthroughs driven by the computer age have reduced the extent of the manual synthesis and testing process at pharmaceutical companies. These breakthroughs are having a positive affect on the cost side of product development, enabling companies to develop new pharmaceuticals that would not have been deemed possible a generation ago.

Computer technology is found in virtually every setting, including smokestack industries. The contrast is eye-opening: twenty-first-century technology driving nineteenth-century processes. Companies that have not invested in computers, software, networks, and the related technology are way behind the curve and are quickly falling further behind.

Such quality standards as those encompassed by the International Organization for Standardization (ISO) virtually demand computer control in processing. Companies that expect to sell products and services on an international scale must comply with those standards. ISO standards are very precise in terms of the raw materials used in manufacturing to the performance of the completed product. And it takes technology to do that.

Consider steel manufacturing for example. In the past, literally thousands of people were required to operate a steel mill, from assembling the raw materials, processing them in the furnace, treating or forming the end products, to shipping them to customers. In today's minimills, a computer determines the mixture of ingredients, checks the process at various stages of production, makes adjustments where necessary, assesses the finished products, and directs the finished products to their destinations. As a result, steel manufacturers produce a consistent, higher-quality product with less potential for human error with just a handful of computer operators to oversee the entire process, versus the labor-intensive methods of the past. It's automation, not manual labor. Instead of many people each doing a job, one or a few people do many jobs via technology.

Computers are increasingly at work in the automobile industry as well, shortening development and production cycle times. Supercomputers allow auto makers to test their designs without having to build expensive and time-consuming clay models. The computers are able to simulate everything from crash test data to the ergonomics of the interior, and allow companies to use common parts in multiple models, thereby reducing costs even further.

Car models that were once extensively redesigned every seven years on average before the advent of computers are now redesigned in less than four years. These improvements have precipitated price decreases to consumers for comparably equipped vehicles, while improving operating margins for the manufacturers.

The Internet is even changing the way vehicles are sold. Buyers who research their prospective vehicles on the Internet know the vehicle's invoice price, dealer incentives, and dealer holdbacks from the manufacturer before they ever walk into a showroom. That is, if they even decide to visit a showroom, because it is now possible to order vehicles over the Internet.

Technology companies themselves have become leaders in cyber business. Dell Computer Corp. and Compaq Computer Corp., for example, operate websites on the Internet where buyers can specify the features they want on their computers. The customer places the order via a mouse click, and the computer is built to customized specifications. The result is a satisfied customer and little or no finished-product inventory.

Technology producers are beneficiaries of their own advances. Because developments occur so quickly, products tend to become obsolete not long after they have been released. This means that customers have to upgrade equipment or buy replacement equipment and technology.

In an earlier era, planned obsolescence was the object of severe criticism. Manufacturers were castigated for deliberately selling products that had to be replaced at higher cost. Technology, however, has changed this, and replacement typically costs less than the original acquisition and has more features. Consequently, consumers are willing to buy the latest

FIGURE 7-1

Microprocessor Advances

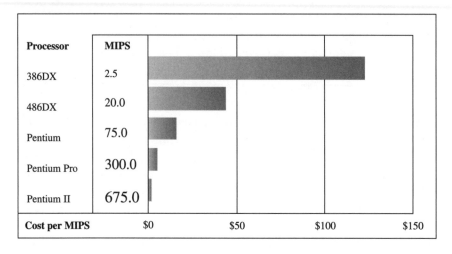

Processor	MIPS			
386DX	2.5			
486DX	20.0			
Pentium	75.0			
Pentium Pro	300.0			
Pentium II	675.0			
Cost per MIPS	$0	$50	$100	$150

versions. Nowhere is this fact more clear than in the price of micro-processors, as Fig. 7-1 illustrates.

Although the absolute cost of processors is higher than when the 386DX was first introduced, the cost on a capability basis has dropped dramatically from $120 per million instructions per second (MIPS) to less than $1. The price decline is a benefit both to technology producers and technology users. The producers generate new sales and revenue, while users acquire more power at less cost.

The majority of computer-based technology firms have been in business for only a short time as compared to conventional industry sectors. Several of the oldest among them have a history of a quarter-century or less. While most are still experiencing the growing pains associated with any new industry or company, some have passed through that stage.

Compaq, Intel Corporation, and Microsoft are examples of companies that have worked through the growing-pain stage of development and have established themselves as solid players in the technology market. These companies have become the industry leaders because they drive technology and the industry.

Today, it is the Internet-oriented companies that are in the growing-pain stage. Not all of them will survive, and there will be much shakeout.

Those that appear to have the strongest potential for surviving and growing are such companies as Yahoo! and Amazon.com.

Although the technology industry is relatively new, considerable consolidation has already occurred. Probably the most significant to date is America Online's acquisition of Netscape Communications Corporation. USRobotics was acquired by 3Com Corp. in June 1997. Investors can expect to see continuing consolidation in the technology sector as small, fragmented entities combine to create new giants. As one company develops a better technology, it may absorb its competition or force it out of business.

Consolidation is driven, to an extent, by the rapid advances in technology itself. Companies with in-demand products one year may see themselves passed by competitors the following year. Hayes Corporation is a prime example of this type shakeout where rapid advances overtake technology companies. Hayes literally invented the modem, allowing computers to link over telephone lines. The modem is the springboard to the Internet and the World Wide Web. Other companies entered the modem market and, because of a combination of circumstances, not the least involving advances in technology, Hayes fell behind the industry and ultimately filed for bankruptcy protection. The company whose invention created the industry fell to its innovative competitors.

Investors have seen technology-related companies, with no history of profitable performance, come on the market. The shares are bid up in a sort of buying frenzy, in large part because of some investors' conviction that any technology company is a wealth engine, e.g., Amazon.com and Yahoo! Later, the shares plummet back to earth, often with frightening speed. After all, technology companies are not immune from the management and investment winds that have blown through companies in other sectors.

The technology stocks of the late 1990s are following a pattern established by the biotechnology companies of the early 1990s. In 1990–91, for example, 101 biotech companies made initial public offerings. By 1999, stocks of 44 were still trading. Today's tech stocks are in the concept phase, as were their biotech predecessors a decade ago: offering promise but not necessarily earnings. As they move into the operating phase, some high-tech companies will fall by the wayside, others will be absorbed by other firms, and a few will survive to maturity.

Some companies' management tools and management styles have not evolved to the point where leadership fully understands that developments can adversely affect the enterprise. IBM, although acknowledged as an industry and stock market leader, is an example of a technology company that went through trying times. After missing the PC boat, the company reinvented itself, returning to a position of prominence not only in the industry, but also in stock market performance.

Since Louis Gerstner became chief executive officer in 1993, IBM has recovered markedly as a company and as a stock. Adjusted for splits, IBM's stock peak in 1987 was $87.375 per share. The low, in August 1993, was $20.50. At year-end 1998, the price had risen to $184.375 a share, as shown in Fig. 7-2.

Investing in a computer is a lot less expensive than adding a new employee to staff and is just one of the reasons that companies across all industries continue to invest in technology. The decline in hardware and software prices, along with increased reliability and a better trained workforce, also drive the use of technology. As computers take over redundant and routine tasks, they continue to free up employees to create the value-added components necessary to grow a business. Following the turn of the century, there will be a virtual explosion in technology not only in the United States, but also internationally.

FIGURE 7-2

IBM's Golden Gerstner Years

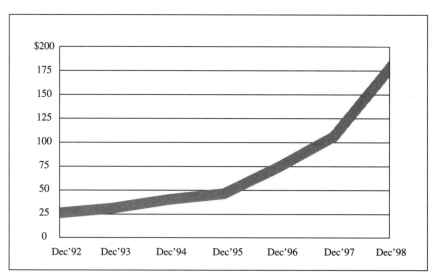

HEALTH CARE

As the American population ages and the baby boom generation begins to retire, an increasing amount of health-care dollars will be spent on preventive medicine and the use of pharmaceuticals as a low-cost alternative to long-term hospitalization.

Within the health-care sector, we concentrate on pharmaceuticals. The medical products and devices and the hospital management companies have not enjoyed as strong or as consistent earnings growth as pharmaceuticals historically have had. Hospitalization and other traditional therapies are expensive methods of treatment. Pharmaceutical alternatives not only delay or even prevent the onset of some diseases and disabilities, they can also reduce the cost of treatment. On a more human level, the advantages to patients are longer, healthier, more productive, and more enjoyable lives.

We expect pharmaceutical treatment trends to continue well into the twenty-first century as the population ages and an increasing number of dollars is spent on prevention-based drugs. There now are drugs to treat osteoporosis, for example. On the preventive side, that means fewer people in the hospital with broken hips, which tend to afflict older women disproportionately compared with men. That's one small snippet where pharmaceuticals are offsetting some of the more intensive health-care cost problems.

Stocks of pharmaceutical companies have gained significantly since the mid-1990s, spurred in large measure by the failure of the Clinton Administration's health-care reform proposals in 1993–94. At that time, investors were concerned that if enacted, federal health-care proposals would place a cap on pharmaceutical companies' earnings. These investors sold pharmaceutical shares in anticipation falling profits. Once the specter of reform lifted from the market, stocks rebounded in the expectation of solid earnings growth free of government involvement.

Pharmaceutical manufacturers have enjoyed increases in revenue and earnings and are making increasing commitments to research and development. Many drug companies target their research and development costs as a percentage of sales. As sales continue to increase, so does the amount spent on research and development. Pharmaceuticals are also intensifying their focus on cost containment, as new technology to develop and test new compounds reduces labor costs.

With the consistency of the earnings that many pharmaceutical companies are reporting, not to mention the new products that they are introducing across the health-care spectrum, we believe that this sector has a strong potential for high return. In addition, the FDA is becoming more accommodative in allowing pharmaceutical companies to label products for use in diseases or disorders for which the products were not originally intended. That, of course, expands the market for a product originally designed for one purpose and subsequently approved for use in another.

Merck & Co., Inc.'s Zocor is a prime example of a drug that was approved by the FDA for additional uses. Zocor was originally approved as a cholesterol-lowering drug. In April 1998, the FDA approved its use to reduce the risk of strokes, opening a new market for the drug and enhancing revenue prospects. Eli Lilly and Company's osteoporosis drug, Evista, also was approved by the FDA for a label change, which allows the company to refer to studies that show that the drug is associated with a reduced risk of breast cancer.

Under some circumstances, a pharmaceutical company is able to extend patent protection, thus assuring competition-protected sales for the length of the extension. That is an attractive dimension for investors.

Some main pharmaceutical companies have been acquiring firms within the industry or within industry sectors. They also have been taking positions in companies at the leading edge of technology and development, such as firms conducting research into genetics.

Manufacturers also have added distributors to their roster of business holdings. Merck's acquisition of Medco, for example, allowed the acquiring company's distribution arm to add to its market base while increasing efficiency. The company also is able to work on a much more global scale.

Many pharmaceutical companies have equity stakes or some sort of investment in start-up and biotechnology companies. If any of these small, niche operations makes an unparalleled breakthrough, it can mean significant gains not only for health care and for the discovering company, but also for the large-capitalization company that helped fund the breakthrough.

Entremed, for example, is developing compounds that kill certain forms of cancer by cutting off the supply of blood to their growth. These compounds, which are complex and difficult to replicate in sufficient quantities, are undergoing further tests on human subjects. If the results stand, they would be a boon to cancer patients, the company itself, and its investors. One of those investors is Bristol-Myers Squibb Company, which owns approximately 7 percent of Entremed.

It doesn't make economic or human resource sense for large companies to conduct research into the universe of diseases and disorders. The small, special-focus companies can do that a lot better by concentrating on specific areas. They work on their specialties, then they team with the large companies to produce and market the product. In some instances, the large company will acquire the small firm, merging it into an operation that already enjoys the advantages of scale.

The United States has become a worldwide leader in pharmaceuticals. There is also a great deal more emphasis in the United States than almost anywhere in the world on pharmaceuticals and drug-based therapies as a result of the free market being allowed to work more effectively than in Europe or the Far East. In Europe, the health care industry is far more regulated and the prices charged for pharmaceuticals are less than in the United States. Those price controls tend to stifle innovation, as companies are less able to recover their costs in a timely fashion.

Many companies have been reluctant to market in the Far East for fear of losing control over their products. The countries in that region, however, are evolving into promising growth markets for pharmaceutical companies as their legal systems begin to recognize patents and developer rights. Consequently, the pharmaceutical industry is going global, with positive implications for medicine and for investors.

As a wealthy country, the United States as a whole can afford to spend more on health care than can some other countries, particularly developing countries. As those countries' wealth begins to catch up with the United States, spending on health care is likely to increase.

FINANCIAL SERVICES

The baby boomers are beginning to reach the "sweet spots" in their careers. They're in the high-paying jobs. They've been in business or their professions for 20 to 25 years. They're at their peak earning years. They're able to save an increasing proportion of their earnings, and they're trying to be efficient in their finances. The financial sector is going to be a major beneficiary of the baby boomers' hitting their prime in the earning cycle. The principal components of the financial services sector are banks, insurance companies, and brokerages.

The late-stage baby boomers (those born during 1946 to 1950) are becoming empty-nesters. They don't have to save for a down payment on a first house, pay for the kids' orthodontia or piano lessons, or put the kids through college. Earnings previously used to pay for these things are now available for saving and investment for later-life items: travel, second home, better car, and most important, retirement. Disposable income is higher.

That's where the financial sector enters the picture. Late-stage baby boomers are concerned that Social Security is not going to provide the level of income that they had imagined earlier in life. They realize that they're going to have to fund a major portion of their retirement years if they're going to maintain the lifestyle they now enjoy or that they envision in retirement. They realize that they need to plant some seeds in the form of assets for harvesting in the years ahead.

Company stocks in the banking, insurance, and brokerage fields will benefit tremendously from this trend and are preparing to handle a large portion of those investment dollars by expanding the services they offer to savers and investors.

As the first stop for most paychecks, banks anticipate taking advantage of their entry-point position to capture a portion of those savings and investments through their own or allied services. Insurance companies provide the vehicle for baby boomers to protect their growing assets in the form of life, health, disability, long-term care, property, and liability coverage. All these factors are a concern to the baby boomers as they accumulate assets. Brokerages also are taking major steps to broaden the range of alternatives for customers to invest in both taxable and tax-sheltered accounts.

The two major sources from which financial institutions, banks especially, generate revenues are interest income and fees. The interest side is a function of the spread between the income the company can generate from its own investment earnings, primarily in the form of loans, and the rate it pays depositors. Banks have become less susceptible to the changes in interest rates that helped to cause the collapse of the savings and loan institutions in the 1980s.

Congress had created an unintended problem when it passed legislation lifting the restrictions on interest rates that banks and savings and loans could pay depositors in an effort to stem the flow of deposits to other institutions. The thrift institutions raised the interest rates that they paid to depositors, often to double-digit levels, in an effort to keep funds within their own institutions. Unfortunately, thrifts were earning interest on mortgages and other long-term fixed-rate loans made before deregulation at lower levels than they were paying. Obviously, paying 10 percent interest on deposits and earning 6 percent on loans is not a recipe for financial success.

Today, banks and other financial institutions manage their short- and long-term interest exposure through hedging techniques that help to insulate interest income. They invest in derivative instruments, which essentially lock in profitable spreads at the inception of the loans they make to borrowers. The lenders match long-term assets with long-term liabilities, and short-term assets with short-term liabilities to prevent the sort of imbalances that led to the financial turbulence of the late 1980s and early 1990s.

The real driver of future earnings growth for financial services companies will be noninterest income. Fees charged for mortgages, credit cards, automated teller machines, and investment management, among others, provide transaction-based revenue that has the added benefit of no credit risk.

Much has changed in the world since the passage of the Glass-Steagall Act in 1934. This law placed severe restrictions on the businesses in which banks were allowed to engage. For instance, banks were prohibited from underwriting securities. As the financial services industry underwent a wave of consolidations, beginning in the late 1980s, regulators took a more permissive view, resulting in de facto repeal of Glass-Steagall. Although some structures might be somewhat unwieldy, banks are now allowed to own brokerage houses and other financial intermediaries and vice versa.

The financial services consolidation wave reached a zenith in 1998 with the combination of the former Citicorp and Travelers Insurance Group to form Citigroup. This new company combined strong revenue sources with a wide-ranging customer base. In addition to economies of scale, Citigroup enjoys the advantages of cross-marketing to customers. A Travelers Insurance policyholder may become a Citibank lending customer. A Citibank mortgage holder becomes a prospect for a Travelers insurance policy. A Salomon Smith Barney client may transfer assets to and from a Citibank account. The combination creates cross-selling opportunities with a global reach, which results in new sources of fee-based income that the pre-merger entities did not enjoy.

The companies taking advantage of these developments are forming revenue and earnings synergies greater than the sum of their parts. Citigroup is the type of financial services company that is going to thrive in the twenty-first century environment.

Banks outside of the United States, of course, did not operate under the Glass-Steagall restrictions, which gave them significant advantages in international finance. With the blurring of lines among products, the financial services firms have had to become competitive, not only within the industry sector, but also against international giants.

Today, federal and state governments have recognized those pressures and have begun to regulate in terms of worldwide competitiveness versus their previous focus on only the domestic market. That has freed financial services companies to enter new markets through mergers and acquisitions that were previously prohibited.

MARKET SECTOR PERFORMANCE

We have organized market sectors into three categories. From those that we expect superior performance, we select core holdings. Those with above average performance, but slightly less growth, can still complement a portfolio. The balance are the underperformers. Although there are other market sectors in which we believe price appreciation is likely, they do not exhibit the same high growth rates we foresee for pharmaceuticals, technology, and financial services. For example, with the globalization of the economy, new markets will open in the consumer sector, particularly as affluence grows in the Third World.

Some American companies already have taken steps to tap these international markets. In the early 1980s, it would have been unheard of for McDonald's Corporation to be selling hamburgers and french fries in Moscow. Nevertheless, McDonald's is among the increasing number of American companies seeking to take advantage of developing markets.

Major telephone companies, in particular such long distance providers as AT&T Corp. and MCI WorldCom Inc., are becoming more like technology companies. Growth is coming from such nontraditional sources as Internet access, data communications, and wireless services. The telephone companies are spending heavily on new technology to keep up with demand.

Companies such as Lucent Technologies Incorporated and Cisco Systems, Inc., provide the equipment to meet this growing demand. Lucent and industry sources estimated in 1997 that more than 2.7 trillion e-mails were sent, 900 million voice mail messages were left each business day, and Internet traffic continued to double every 100 days. Internet traffic is tripling each year and is expected to overtake the volume of voice traffic by 2005.

Utilities—electricity, natural gas, and local telephone—while not a fast-growing sector, generate income through relatively high dividends. This feature, however, is becoming less attractive, especially in light of the cuts in the federal long-term capital gains tax rate, which confer more control to the investor in timing taxable events.

There is considerable consolidation taking place in utilities, and this trend is likely to continue, largely because of the fragmentation of the industry. Regulatory bodies are easing their restrictions, contributing to consolidation. Because of increasing competition stemming from federal deregulation, utilities are facing stiff pricing pressures. The consumer should benefit from the price competition, increasing disposable income for the baby boomers and easing financial strains on the already retired.

As consumers reap the benefit of price competition in the form of reduced expenses, they will place a portion of their new-found disposable income into investments, including stocks. Increased demand for stocks should invigorate the market.

In contrast to the telecommunications sector, the energy sector is in a slow-growth phase. For oil producers, for example, low commodity prices are driving consolidation as a means to cut costs. This trend is exhibited in the announcement of the merger between Exxon Corporation and Mobil Corporation and the merger of Amoco and British Petroleum. The Exxon-Mobil merger reconstitutes a majority of John D. Rockefeller's Standard Oil Trust.

Basic industries are dependent upon two factors to grow revenue and earnings: growing industrial output and/or pricing power. Commodity inflation is virtually nonexistent, and many commodities have actually dropped in price. Global demand, meanwhile, is stymied by problems in the Far East.

Abundant supply and industry globalization have affected hard goods such as steel, copper, iron ore, coal, paper, chemicals. Pricing flexibility and leverage are all but nonexistent. Basic industries, then, do not have the factors they need to increase revenues and earnings, neither growth nor pricing power. Companies in these industries typically lack specific competitive advantages that mark firms in technology, telecommunications, and pharmaceuticals.

The last sector of the S&P is transportation. Besides being a relatively small sector, transportation tends to be cyclical. The rails and shipping companies are undergoing consolidation in the United States, and the airlines are consolidating or forming operating relationships that are falling just short of consolidation. Consequently, the air travel component of the transportation sector is undergoing a globalization of its own.

We believe that technology, health care, and financial are the three sectors that will enjoy growth rates in excess of the overall market, even beyond the time frame that we have set for the DJIA to hit 40,000. These are the sectors that will drive the future, because they are the sectors that drive the way people live their lives and how companies do business.

BEYOND THE BABY BOOMERS

Concern that the markets will implode when the baby boomers begin to withdraw their building wealth is unfounded. Not all of their resources will be withdrawn at once. Instead, retiring boomers will extract their wealth on an orderly basis. Growth of assets will still be important to maintain the lifestyles of retirees who are expected to live much longer than their counterparts of a few decades ago. Further, those still in the workforce will seek their own investment vehicles, causing generational redeployment of assets that will continue the cycle.

The wealth that is being created by the baby boom generation will flow to succeeding generations. The new owners will follow patterns similar to those currently in effect. They will take the wealth that they inherit and, in turn, commit to investments to assure their future prosperity. Obviously, entities other than the owners will also benefit: cultural and charitable organizations through increased contributions and government at various levels through increased tax revenues, among others. The cycle will simply continue.

The baby boomers are learning from the lessons that those retiring in the late 1990s and early twenty-first century failed to learn. They and succeeding generations must invest to ensure their own futures.

CHAPTER 8

Investment Themes for the Next 20 Years

Fewer than one in 100 Americans owned stocks in 1929. Near the close of the twentieth century, however, almost 60 percent of the population owned stocks either directly or indirectly. Direct stock ownership means that individuals own the stocks in their own names or that the stocks are held for them in "street name." In the former case, the individuals have possession of the stock certificates, which are registered with the issuing company in the owners' names. In the latter case, brokerages or other intermediaries electronically register shares that they hold on the owners' behalf. The owners receive any dividends and other distributions and are entitled to vote on issues presented to all shareholders.

An investor who owns H. J. Heinz Company shares in street name, for example, still receives not only quarterly and annual reports, but the opportunity to vote on shareholder issues as well. The company also offers the street-name investor special premiums, such as a computer mouse pad, a model of a vintage truck, and a Charlie the Tuna beanbag toy.

Indirect stock ownership means that an individual owns stocks through mutual funds or such retirement vehicles as an individual retirement account (IRA), a 401(k), and similar plans. In both instances, the investors receive regular reports and statements from which they may calculate the performance of their investments. Today, there are more than 7,000 mutual funds of all stripes, plus an uncountable number of such other vehicles as annuities, corporate-sponsored stock purchase plans, and investment clubs.

There are plenty of incentives to encourage people to invest in stocks and stock-holding instruments. Employee stock buying plans, for example, encourage workers to take a financial stake in their companies. Stock grants and bonuses add to employees' stakes in their companies as well as exposing them to the equity markets.

Since the advent of 401(k) plans in 1981, the dramatic shift from defined-benefit to defined-contribution retirement plans has encouraged people to investigate investment alternatives, including common stocks. Under defined-benefit plans, the sponsor promises to pay a fixed amount on a regular basis to the beneficiary. In defined-contribution plans, the amount deposited into the program is fixed, not the benefit, which will vary depending on the portfolio performance. Employees conduct their own research, learn about the stock market, and make their investment decisions based on the information they have gathered.

For such employees, stock ownership becomes an enterprise. There is, of course, an element of risk, but such shareholders realize that they're not alone, that their families, friends, and colleagues have a stake as well. That has no effect on risk for individual investors, of course, although they realize that they are sharing in the risk with other investors.

Stock ownership, moreover, has become a very pervasive issue, with people discussing the pros and cons of investing, the forms of ownership, and the investment merits of individual issuers. The effect of all this cross-communication is the ever-growing number of households investing in the market: 59.8 percent as of 1998. The level of sophistication among American stock investors may be gauged by individual investors' reactions to pullbacks. There is clear evidence that they do not sell in panic; rather, at those times, they buy stocks or the mutual funds that own stocks.

This impressive increase in stock ownership among Americans over the course of 70 years demonstrates that those shareholders realize that if they are to achieve their investment objectives, they must be willing to accept the risk that accompanies stock ownership.

RISK AND RETURN

It's trite but true that reward is earned in proportion to risk. Sometimes it's stated: no risk, no reward. For investors, the reward takes the form of returns, or price increases and dividends, which raise the value of their holdings. There's a vast difference between a gamble and a risk. A gamble involves long shots with slim chances of success. Risks, on the other hand, are components that the investor measures before making a decision.

In his book *Against the Gods: The Remarkable Story of Risk,* Peter Bernstein eloquently defines risk this way: "The word 'risk' derives from the early Italian *'risicare,'* which means 'to dare.' In this sense risk is a choice rather than a fate. The actions we dare to take, which depend on how free we are to make choices, are what the story of risk is all about."[1]

In baseball, the player on first base takes into account myriad factors before deciding whether to steal second base: the pitcher and the catcher, the hitter at the plate, even the score, the inning, and the ball-and-strike count. If the situation justifies taking the risk, the runner heads toward second with the pitch. Similarly, gauging and managing risk are elemental factors that investors must account for in making decisions concerning their investments. Assuming too much or too little risk can place the outcome in serious jeopardy.

Risk is defined differently by individual investors than it is by institutional money managers. The money managers usually consider risk as volatility, embedded in such terms as variance from the mean and standard deviation. Individual investors often define risk as the chance of losing money. It should be understood that risk determines not simply returns in the short term but, more important, in the long term. Over longer periods of time, the greater the risk, the greater the return. That axiom is relevant because the market demands a greater rate of return from financial instruments that are more volatile and variable than are supposedly safe financial assets, such as Treasury bills and bank deposits. Let's see why these safe assets aren't so safe.

There are several principal forms of risk entailed in investing. Market risk refers to the potential for a decline in a portfolio's value when prices fall. It also is termed "systemic risk," or risk that cannot be avoided. It's the price of playing the game, and it is this type of risk that comes to most people's minds when they consider the stock market.

Throughout history, however, whenever the overall market falls, as measured by the generally accepted indexes and averages, it has always returned to its earlier highs. More important, the market has gone on unfailingly to forge new highs. Over the years, several declines have exceeded 20 percent in market measures, the generally accepted definition of a bear market. They all were short-term events in the long-term rising trend of the market.

---

[1]Bernstein, Peter L. 1998. *Against the Gods: The Remarkable Story of Risk.* New York: John Wiley & Sons, Inc., p. 8.

Inflation is probably the misunderstood culprit in eroding wealth creation through investment. Everyone realizes that a dollar does not go as far today as it did 10 or 20 years ago. Therefore, investors have to provide for this erosion: either the income or the value of the investment has to increase as fast or faster than the rate of inflation.

The effects of inflation can be devastating over time, reducing purchasing power considerably and, consequently, style and quality of life, if assets haven't grown at a commensurate or higher rate. Because of inflation, cash over time loses purchasing power. Assuming a 5 percent inflation rate, purchasing power is cut in half in 14 years. Such cash-like investments as short-term Treasury bills, bank savings accounts, and money market funds tend to move along at roughly the rate of inflation. They may keep pace, but they won't dramatically outpace inflation, thus failing to significantly enhance quality of life or lifestyle.

If an investor's time horizon is 10 years or longer, therefore, the riskiest investments are cash and short-term interest vehicles. That is the cost of not being in the stock market: missing out on high stock returns, because capital was invested in very liquid, typically short-term investments. In investment circles, that's considered opportunity cost.

Business risk, or stock-specific risk, deals with the invested company continuing as a going concern. This entails taking steps to maintain and even to increase business advantages over competitors. The company must be capable of adapting its business model to maintain profit margins and sales growth in order to keep the firm on a path of prosperity.

Hayes Corp. is an example of stock-specific risk. Thanks to its inventions and discoveries involving modems, at one time Hayes was the undisputed leader in its industry. The company, however, did not maintain a position of leadership. Other companies perfected the modem beyond the point that Hayes was able. Subsequently, Hayes encountered product, industry, and financial difficulty, ultimately filing for bankruptcy protection and effectively going out of business in early 1999.

Another type of risk is specific to certain industry groups. If interest rates rise, stocks in general do poorly, but bank and insurance stocks tend to perform worse than the overall market. If oil prices rise, integrated oil companies and oil service stocks do well, while airlines and railroads whose earnings are, in part, dependent on the cost of fuel, tend to suffer.

All risks, except for market risk, can be managed through diversification. Stock market risk cannot be completely eliminated, but it can be reduced by owning stock in companies in different industry sectors that are not closely correlated.

Summing up the role that risk plays in generating wealth, Leonard Reinhart, chief executive officer of Lockwood Financial, comments, "I've never met anyone who became wealthy—not who inherited wealth but who earned it—who did not take a lot of risk.

"Within any wealthy family, somewhere along the line someone took risk to earn that wealth. Once that wealth is earned, the risk factor lessens. The object then becomes to preserve that wealth.

"Most people, however, are not in that category," he drolly observes.[2]

Investors should understand that they are not alone when it comes to risk. All their fellow investors, whether large institutions or individuals with small amounts of money in stocks, share the same risk factors. The difference among them is the range of experience with risk.

DETERMINING RISK TOLERANCE

Markets, of course, go up and they come down. In the twentieth century, there have been 50 declines in stock prices of 10 percent or more, which averages about one every other year. There were pullbacks in 1990, 1994, 1996, 1997, and 1998. Each time, the market recovered to set new highs as measured by the Dow Jones Industrial Average. Shakeouts are not uncommon and are, in fact, good for the market. They present opportunities for investors to make initial purchases at less cost than at stocks' high points. Or they may add to their holdings, often at prices lower than they originally paid.

Before committing funds to any stock, however, investors must determine the level of risk that they are willing to accept with investments. How well are you, as an investor, able to withstand the sometimes-violent volatility in the stock market over the short term? The answer requires a certain introspection and self-analysis. Investors should analyze their own personalities to decide how much risk they are willing to accept in return for the potential of increasing the value of their portfolios. There is no quick answer to the question of how much risk an investor can tolerate. It's not like taking a patient's temperature by inserting a thermometer under the tongue. There is no formula that can be applied. There is no one-size-fits-all. Each investor must analyze the various

---

[2]Reinhart, Leonard. 1998. Telephone interview by J. Patrick Donlon. Snyder, New York. 15 December.

components that help measure individual tolerance to risk. There are several questions to ask yourself before committing funds to the stock market.

The first and most obvious question concerns your goals. These might be tangible goals, such as a new home or a college education for a child, or intangible goals, such as security or status, which may be more difficult to quantify in a meaningful way. Your answers to the following questions affect your allocation between high dividend stocks and low or no dividend stocks, or the overall allocation among stocks, bonds, and cash.

- Are these goals very important to you or less important?
- Are these goals short-term or long-term in nature?
- How much current income do you require?
- What is your worst case outcome, especially in the short run?
- Do you have sufficient resources outside stocks to handle a 20 percent drop in the market without affecting your standard of living?
- How important are your equity holdings to your overall financial condition?

Investors who thoughtfully answer these questions will be better able to ascertain their personal levels of risk tolerance. Investors educated in the market understand that although the value of such investments might decline periodically, the value also is likely to increase over time. Over time, these increases far exceed the decreases, which can lead to a more comfortable tolerance for higher risk.

Most people have had savings accounts at some point. They grew accustomed and comfortable with seeing small increases each time interest was credited to their accounts. In determining personal levels of risk, an individual investor might consider the reactions if the number in that savings account declined from one month to the next, or even over several months.

Some investors become easily rattled when they observe on their monthly statements that the values of their portfolios are 10 percent less than the previous month. Nevertheless, downturns, even bear markets where values drop by approximately 20 percent or more from their highs, tend to be compressed, as shown in Fig. 8-1. Bull markets tend to be longer, although not in a straight, upward line.

It boils down to experiencing personally the various fluctuations in the market and reacting to them. This includes experiences in investment

FIGURE 8-1

Duration of Bear Markets

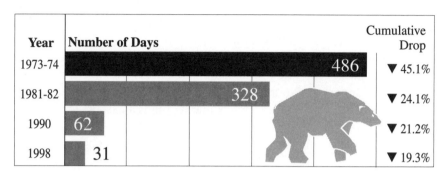

Year	Number of Days	Cumulative Drop
1973-74	486	▼ 45.1%
1981-82	328	▼ 24.1%
1990	62	▼ 21.2%
1998	31	▼ 19.3%

clubs, reading reports from employer-sponsored investment plans and IRA accounts, and managing an inheritance.

In entering the stock market, an investor must understand that the reward potential is much greater than the savings account can return, although the risk potential also may be greater. It helps not to get to caught up in short-term market gyrations, but to focus on the goals that led you to the stock market in the first place. After all, most people do not check the value of their houses, boats, or cars on a daily basis. Why should it be different for an asset that generally gains in value over time, versus assets that decline in value, such as cars and boats? Indeed, Americans do seem to be growing more comfortable with the realities of investing, given the increasing percentage of households that own stock investments, either directly or indirectly.

RISK AND TIME

Personal risk tolerance depends on an investor's temperament and time horizon. A diversified portfolio creates a platform for investors to commit assets at a risk level with which they feel comfortable, based on the length of time they expect the assets to grow before harvesting them. Obviously, investors within a few years of retirement have different ideas of their levels of risk than investors who are just beginning to make commitments to the market.

One of the fallacies of investing is that the minute people retire, they should no longer take on risk in their portfolios but should convert to a 100 percent fixed-income structure. This may have been true decades ago when people did not live long after retirement, but today when people often live 20 years or more after retirement, money must continue to grow. Further, I've personally found that many clients generally recognize the benefits of stock ownership and do not change their investment portfolios substantially after they retire.

There is an inverse relationship between risk and time. Portfolios, therefore, can be structured to include components invested for growth, safety, and income. For short periods of time, the lowest risk is in cash and cash-like investments, such as money market funds and short-term bonds. For the mutual fund investor, balanced funds provide an element of safety, as well. The riskiest investments for the short term are stocks and equity mutual funds, especially those invested in international and emerging markets.

For the long term, however, the return spectrum reverses. The greatest risk over the long term is the opportunity cost of not being in the stock market. The lowest risk for trying to meet and beat inflation, given a 10-year-plus time horizon, is in equity markets, just the opposite of the short-term risk factor. The highest risk over the long term is in the lowest volatility investment: money market funds. These investors are surrendering the greatest potential for growth by investing in money market funds for the long term.

The adage in investing is that the best time to get into the market was 20 years ago. The second best time is today. It's important to begin investing as soon as possible, to stay invested despite stock market gyrations, and to not lose sight of the objective over time.

Investors in their twenties or thirties who haven't had much experience either in the market or with risk, might consider dividing their investment funds into categories that span the risk line. They can then start investing on a regularly scheduled basis, even via mutual funds. It's not important that the amount seems small to them. The critical element is to stick with the schedule.

For example, I'll illustrate the powerful effect of compound interest for an investor who begins small but continues to make annual contributions to a portfolio. This investor, age 25, begins with $2,000 in the stock market, in individual stocks or in a mutual fund. The investor adopts a strategy known as dollar-cost averaging. The number of dollars invested each year will remain the same, but the number of shares acquired will vary according to the price of the shares each time that they are purchased. Assume that the investor makes a $2,000 contribution each year at the beginning of the year and earns 10 percent each year on the investment. At the end of 20 years, that $2,000 annual investment will exceed $114,500. At the end of 30 years, it will be worth in excess of $325,000. At the end of 40 years, when the investor turns 65 years old, the portfolio will be worth more than $875,000. Not bad, considering that the investor put to work $80,000 over 40 years.

Investors may diversify their portfolios among various asset classes, but the overwhelming majority should be in equities. Investment options include large cap (capitalization) stocks, small cap stocks, growth stocks, value stocks, and international stocks. There also should be much smaller proportions of long-term bonds, short-term bonds, certificates of deposit, and cash.

Investors may devote longer-term money to international and emerging markets stocks, as well as domestic small and large capitalization stocks and/or funds, while short-term funds are placed in short-term bonds and money market funds. The advantage of diversification is that the portfolio is not a well-oiled machine. The parts will not make a synchronized move in the same direction. There will be variations within and among markets.

Take 1998 for example. While the Dow Jones Industrial Average (DJIA) was up more than 16 percent and the S&P 500 was up almost 27 percent, the Mexican Bolsa (Mexico's major stock market) was down more than 24 percent, and Brazil was lower by more than 33 percent. Meanwhile, the Nikkei in Japan was down less than 10 percent. If an investor is staying true to the self-adopted discipline and the allocation strategy, that individual is essentially buying the same stocks or mutual funds as the year before. For the international component, the investor is buying at a significant discount price from the prior year. The investor can remain confidence that given enough time, the international stocks and funds will go up as the companies they represent react to constantly changing circumstances.

Those circumstances include the strength of the domestic economy and the strength of the currency, versus other currencies, to name merely a few of the variables. After several years of consistently following the established pattern of dollar-cost averaging, the portfolio is likely to show positive results. Over time, as the different components of the portfolio show different results, several options open to the investor.

One option is to continue to allocate investment funds into the components of the portfolio as in the past. For example, allocate 25 percent to large cap growth, 25 percent to large cap value, 25 percent to small cap growth, and 25 percent to international stocks and mutual funds. Another option is to invest more in the portfolio components that are down or have not risen as much as other components. This will effectively re-balance the portfolio without having to incur substantial transaction costs that eat into portfolio returns.

For example, take a portfolio whose owner has seen the value of stocks increase 10 percent past allocation and bonds fall 5 percent below allocation. This investor may bring the bond portion back to standard by investing new funds there or by selling some stocks and reinvesting the proceeds in bonds, bringing both back into line.

The key to financial success, as it is in every other endeavor, is to maintain the discipline of doing it over and over again. Constant and continual investing, whether the market is up or down, will prevent knee-jerk reactions and increase the likelihood that financial goals are met. Psychologically, most investors have difficulty in continuing to hold a poorly performing investment when other investments in the portfolio are doing well. In fact, this discipline can be viewed as a type of homemade insurance, a policy that grows in value over time and allows the owner of the policy to sleep well at night.

As with any insurance policy, however, it should be reviewed periodically and adapted to meet new circumstances. Investments and allocations should be changed when goals change or as goals become closer to being realized. At some point, perhaps a few years away from paying college tuition, buying a vacation home, or funding retirement expenses, the portfolio allocation could be changed to ensure the necessary funds are available to meet those commitments.

TIME VERSUS TIMING

Our investment philosophy takes risk well into account. I believe, generally, that investors should focus on the long term and make commitments to first-quality issues. They should allow those commitments to grow undisturbed, irrespective of market fluctuations.

For time horizons greater than five years, I favor long-term, growth-oriented, large capitalization, blue chip companies. Why? Many of these companies have been part of the market for decades or even a century or longer. They have weathered world wars, oil embargoes, presidential assassinations and resignations, and economic depressions and recessions. Others, while relatively recent additions to the market, display the characteristics that we seek. Those are the stocks that are going to withstand the storms in the market.

Our firm calls them Face of the Earth companies. Their stocks provide investors peace of mind. Examples are AT&T Corp., American

Express Company, Bristol-Myers Squibb Company, Citigroup, Inc., Exxon Corporation, General Electric Company, Merck & Co., Inc., and Walt Disney Company. Over time, those issues will provide solid returns with acceptable risk. We know that during unsettled market conditions, it is much easier for most investors to hold a select number of solid companies that they believe will be around for a long time than it is to have a number of companies that don't inspire strong, long-term faith.

There is another form of risk that is self-imposed and can easily be avoided. That risk is in attempting to determine the optimal time to buy or to sell stocks in an effort to maximize return. This form of risk closely resembles gambling. It is market timing. When the stock market appears to some investors to be nearing a peak in terms of equity prices, they sell their stocks. They want to be out of the market when it tanks. Similarly, when the market appears to them to be nearing the bottom, they buy. They want to be in the market to take advantage of profit potential when prices rebound.

Such investors are called "market timers." They seek to time their purchases and sales in advance of major moves. Unfortunately for them, market timing has been proved an inefficient and even losing technique in investing. Assume that an investor made a $1,000 investment in the stock market and left it undisturbed between 1978 and 1997. That initial investment would have grown to $21,750. On the other hand, consider the investor who placed $1,000 in the market in 1978, but withdrew the money and reinvested it depending on bullish or bearish sentiments and was out of the market during the 15 months when stocks recorded their biggest advances. The original $1,000 investment would have grown to $6,000, roughly one-third the return earned by leaving the original investment undisturbed. The risk in the market timing strategy is further demonstrated by some simple statistics. Over the past decade, those who were out of the market on the 10 days with the strongest upward price moves cut about one-third off their total returns. Those who missed the top 40 days in the same decade earned a return below that of Treasury bills.

The return on stocks has outpaced that of any other form of investment. According to Ibbotson Associates and the latest data available, stocks, as measured by the S&P 500, returned 11.2 percent between 1925 and 1998. Government bonds provided 5.3 percent, and cash 3.8 percent, as measured by Treasury bills, for the same period.[3] This time span in-

---

[3]Ibbotson Associates. 1999. *Stocks, Bonds, Bills, and Inflation.* Chicago: Ibbotson Associates.

cluded some major disruptions around the globe, even wars. Recall the
tension between China and her neighbors, the collapse of currencies, rev-
olutions, oil-supply crises, and the fall of communism.

Stocks consistently outperform any other asset class over the long
term. It is during the trying and difficult times that investors have to take
into account the trade-off between risk and reward. If investors are willing
to stay the course over the long term in stocks, or at least a portfolio emphasizing stocks, their returns will be the highest among all of the categories of investment instruments.

Some people look back and observe that if only they had invested
some money when a fast-rising issue first came on the market, they would
have a lot more money today. The same holds true when the stock market
stumbled; if they had taken the risk at or near a stock price's low point, their
investments would be worth a great deal more than they would have paid.

Actually, risk is probably the wrong term to use. It is an opportunity
to buy more stock in the companies and mutual funds that the investor already owns or in companies that the investor does not currently own but
has been following for a time.

Although an investor may have missed a previous opportunity,
there is no reason why the investment shouldn't be made now. If an issue
comes on the market that's attractive and fits within the confines of an investor's risk tolerance, it should be considered for purchase. Likewise, if
investors have spotted stocks that they like but not at current prices, they
can bide their time until the prices decline. If the prices don't reach their
targets, they may conclude that the stocks were overpriced for their purposes.

In summary, I urge investors to stay in the market for the long term
and not to attempt to time the market. Even when markets decline, it does
not mean that conditions are inappropriate to invest. It usually means that
conditions are unsettled. Down markets are often an opportunity to buy at
lower prices.

ALLOCATING RISK

Portfolios can be custom-structured to take each individual's risk tolerance into account. An all-equity portfolio, for example, puts investors at
the highest level of short-term volatility but offers the highest potential for
return over the long term. Within this all-equity portfolio, allocations can
be adjusted according to the nature of the securities: small, mid-sized, and
large capitalization stocks; orientations with respect to growth, growth

and income, and income; domestic issues, international stocks, or emerging markets.

Despite the stellar record of past performance, there is no guarantee of a positive future return with stocks. Nevertheless, I believe strongly that this strong, upward performance will continue well into the future, with the Dow hitting 40,000. Although I believe that investors should concentrate on common stocks, bonds can play an important role in a well-diversified portfolio.

With top-quality government bonds, investors are assured of a return based on the coupon interest. A 5 percent coupon bond will return 5 percent each year. However, investors are locked into that return for the length of time that they own the bond. Even with that assured return, a potential problem comes on the horizon as the bond nears maturity. There can be no assurance that the proceeds or the principal from that bond can be invested in a new bond that will yield the same return.

In a declining interest-rate environment, such as in both the early and the late 1990s, intermediate and long-term bonds were yielding rates well below comparable issues of earlier years. Interest rates, as measured by the 30-year Treasury bond, peaked in 1981, just shy of 15 percent. Since then, the trend has been basically downward, with the yield on the 30-year Treasury bond at 5.09 percent at year-end 1998. Another problem with bonds is the potential loss if bonds must be sold before maturity. Bond prices are pegged to the coupon rate or, in the case of a zero-coupon Treasury, are based on an implied rate to yield the stated face value at maturity.

To continue the previous example, consider a bond that yields annual interest of 5 percent of face value. If the investor must sell the bond prior to maturity and the market yields have climbed above 5 percent, the price of the bond will fall and the investor will incur a loss.

Obviously, I've made a very strong case that equities are the place for investors with long-term goals. I am especially convinced of this, in light of the new millennium, the very favorable trends in demographics, the privatization of companies in formerly communist countries, and the opening of markets worldwide.

STOCK CHARACTERISTICS

The companies that we favor have solid, forward-looking management teams, with market-leading products and geographic breadth. In fact, these companies have created business models capable of dealing with the range of unforeseen developments. They've lived through the vagaries that have stymied competitors, even to the point of bringing them down. They know how to manage their businesses to assure prosperity for their companies and for their shareholders.

During the 1997–98 Asian financial crisis, Jack Welch, chairman of General Electric, was asked whether developments would crimp the company's growth expectations. He noted that he and his company had confronted difficulties many times. Those experiences forged confidence in his own abilities and his management team's abilities to deal with the Asian crisis. As a global corporation, he commented, GE is able to source products and raw materials from the countries undergoing deflationary pressures, and at prices lower than the company is accustomed to paying. Meanwhile, GE focuses sales efforts on those countries that continue to do well and invests in those countries where weakness is evident. The company will be able to make acquisitions that will add to its production capacity at costs well below those of replacing current assets or undertaking new construction. In fact, in 1998, GE completed 93 acquisitions, totaling more than $18 billion. In the first seven years of the 1990s, GE spent more than $20 billion in Europe when markets opened up after the collapse of the Berlin Wall.

Welch views the weakness in Asia as an opportunity to replicate the success that the company's investments in Europe have achieved. GE is far from the only company investing overseas, having been joined by such others as Wal-Mart Stores, Inc., United Technologies Corporation, and Merrill Lynch & Co., Inc.

Welch viewed the scenario as one in which a multinational company, such as GE, is able to leverage the company's management experience, skills, and financial resources to its advantage.

I, too, foresee these trends continuing and even accelerating. The GEs of this world are well positioned to take advantage of opportunities. In fact, this is one of the factors driving the mergers of large players in some industries, such as Exxon Corporation and Mobil Corporation in the energy sector. These companies are seeking to maintain and to increase scale, to enhance productivity and efficiency, to create long-term synergies, and to remain competitive on a global scale.

Clearly, I believe in owning those American companies that have a tradition of doing business worldwide and have proved that they know how to do so successfully.

INDIVIDUAL STOCKS VERSUS MUTUAL FUNDS

One question that investors need to consider in developing a portfolio is whether to purchase individual stock and bond issues, mutual funds, or a combination of both. Many of the differences between individual stocks and equity mutual funds are in the areas of diversification, taxes, and fees.

For investors just getting started, it is difficult to achieve sufficient diversification by purchasing individual stocks. Even if an investor were to purchase a few shares in 30 different companies, the transaction costs on a per-share basis would be prohibitive. The downside to owning mutual funds versus individual stocks is related to taxes and fees. A mutual fund distributes all its earnings each year because the fund is taxed only on the earnings that remain in the fund at fiscal year-end. Therefore, earnings are taxed when distributed to the shareholder.

There are two types of distributions to shareholders. The first is a dividend, which covers any dividends and interest the fund has received from the companies in which it has invested during the year. The second is based on capital gains, and is the net from the sale of securities held in the portfolio. Under federal tax regulations, such gains may be short term if the fund had owned the asset for less than one year or long term if held for more than one year.

Mutual funds report to investors whether gains are long or short term. Investors, in turn, report them on their own income tax returns. As of 1999, short-term gains are taxed at the federal level as ordinary income, while long-term gains are taxed at a maximum rate of 20 percent for investors in the 28 percent and above taxable-income brackets. Most states that levy taxes on personal income extend favorable treatment to long-term capital gains in line with federal regulations.

If the mutual fund is not part of a retirement plan or some other tax-deferred program, those distributions are taxable, irrespective of how long the investor has owned shares in the mutual fund. Even if the investor purchased the mutual fund one day before the distribution was made, that investor would receive the full distribution, based on the number of shares owned, and have to report it for tax purposes.

The Internal Revenue Service requires mutual funds to specify in reports to shareholders the amount of distribution that represents long- and short-term capital gains. Shareholders then report long- and short-term distributions separately on their income tax returns.

This should serve as a warning to investors in taxable situations to check on their funds' distribution policies before investing. Investors in individual companies must declare only the cash dividends they receive, and even that can be avoided by pursuing growth companies that do not pay dividends.

An investor in individual companies also has to pay tax on capital gains, but the key difference is the tax is paid at the discretion of the investor. If an investor follows a buy and hold strategy, then capital gains taxes are not paid until the stock is sold, often many years following its purchase. The 20 percent long-term capital gains tax rate is usually less than the investor's earned income tax rate and is an advantage in a buy and hold strategy.

Investors in mutual funds must pay a capital gains tax if they sell their shares at a net asset value higher than their purchase price. Mutual fund investors also are subject to a tax on capital gains if they exchange shares in one mutual fund for shares in another mutual fund, assuming the fund is not held in a tax-deferred account.

An investor in the shares of individual companies typically pays a commission to the broker arranging the transaction, based on the number of shares purchased and the price of each share. Commissions have dropped substantially since the industry was deregulated, with such discount brokers as Charles Schwab & Co. Inc. have appeared on the scene. More recently, commissions have dropped even further with the advent of online trading.

An alternative to commissions for investors in individual securities is a wrap fee, charged on the total asset value of the portfolio. Such wrap fees generally run about 1 percent, payable annually, and cover the costs of trading, reporting, and recordkeeping.

A mutual fund investor may be subject to several fees. There may be front-end fees, deferred sales charges, redemption fees, and exchange fees. These fees are in addition to annual operating expenses. Operating expenses may include management fees paid to the fund's investment advisor and 12b-1 fees to pay for marketing and distribution expenses. Consequently, investors should be aware of their funds' expense ratios.

Despite the tax implications and fees, I recommend mutual funds as a way to start investing in equities. The minimum required is low for many funds, and investors can start with as little as $100 a month, regularly withdrawn from a designated account. As assets grow, supplementing mutual fund holdings with specific stock issues is an excellent way to round out a portfolio and make it more tax-efficient for holdings that are not part of tax-deferred accounts.

CHAPTER 9

Funds for the Future

The stock market offers an opportunity to participate in the wealth creation that I believe will continue well into the next century. Some people, however, have not yet begun to participate even though they realize that investing has the potential for helping them reach a higher standard of living. They are also not certain how and where to get started. These potential investors often feel uncomfortable in dealing with the colossus that their imaginations have built of the financial markets. They may feel that they don't have the financial resources to begin investing to build future wealth. They also have a lot more to do with their time and energy than to pore over reams and screens of facts and figures.

Robert Goodman, managing director/senior economic advisor of Putnam Funds, a well-respected mutual fund company, won't let prospective investors get away with the excuse that they can't find the money or that they don't have the time. "The best way to start investing, typically with someone who has an income, is with setting aside part of the income in a systematic way. It's the tried and true 'pay yourself first.' The easiest way to begin investing is out of cash flow. It doesn't have to be a lot of money."

Goodman says that beginning investors usually find the money if they're willing to impose some self-discipline. If necessary, he recommends substituting a little spending for investing, saying, "People who smoke, or who have smoked, can take the money spent on cigarettes and turn it into the start of an investment program. If they didn't smoke that pack of cigarettes, or they cut back from two packs a day to one," they will have the start of an investment plan. He runs the math: "At, say, $3 per pack, that becomes $90 at the end of a month. Starting at age 20 and continuing through age 65, investing $90 per month in the S&P 500 would amount to more than $1 million.

"People who think they don't make much money spend $90 a month (in the case of the hypothetical smoker). It's an easy way to start, and in the end they'll live long enough to retire." Speaking to the individual investor, he concludes, "Eliminating things that aren't really necessary, or things that are even harmful, can be the starting point of an investment program. It will give you the cash flow that you need."[1]

AN INSTANT PORTFOLIO

So where do novices turn to launch their investment programs, and to make the best decisions they can? How do they determine which stocks, bonds, and other instruments will go into their portfolios? For many, mutual funds may be the answer. Millions of individual investors around the world have effectively hired someone to conduct all of the intensive research and to make the tough decisions in the world of investment alternatives. When an investor makes the first purchase of a mutual fund, he or she creates a portfolio in a single step.

John C. Bogle, founder and senior chairman of Vanguard Group, one of the largest mutual fund companies in the United States, underscores this point. "In my view, attempting to build a lifetime investment program around the selection of a handful of individual securities is, for all but the most exceptional investor, a fool's errand. . . Earning extraordinary returns from the ownership of individual stocks is a high-risk, long-shot bet for most investors. . . For nearly all investors, mutual funds are the most efficient method of achieving that diversification."[2]

Decisions concerning the various investments within a portfolio, as well as when to buy and sell them, become the responsibility of the mutual fund manager or of the fund's management team. Individual investors

---

[1]Goodman, Robert. 1998. Telephone interview by J. Patrick Donlon. Snyder, New York. 8 December.

[2]Bogle, John C. 1994. *Bogle on Mutual Funds*. Burr Ridge, Illinois: Irwin Professional Publishing, p. vii.

can then devote the bulk of their time to other details in their lives. The concept of investing in mutual funds, as opposed to specific stocks, bonds, and other instruments, has found favor among other experts as well, including the venerable Benjamin Graham, pioneer in the value style of investing and mentor to the renowned Warren Buffett, and Jane Bryant Quinn, investment author and syndicated columnist.

In *The Intelligent Investor,* called by Buffett "by far the best book on investing ever written," Graham opined that, "funds in the aggregate have served a useful purpose. They have promoted good habits of savings and investment; they have protected countless individuals against costly mistakes in the stock market; they have brought their participants income and profits commensurate with the overall returns from common stocks."[3]

He summarized his view by noting that on a comparative basis, mutual fund investors over the 10 years preceding publication fared better than the average person who made common stock purchases directly. Today, this is likely as true near the end of the twentieth century as it was in 1950.

More than four decades following publication of the first edition of *The Intelligent Investor,* Quinn repeated the advice. "Good mutual funds give you full-time, professional money management, which you normally cannot do yourself. The managers diversify your investments and balance your risks. Picking stocks individually is a fascinating game, but for the dedicated hobbyist only."[4]

A MUTUAL FUNDS PRIMER

Mutual funds take the money that their customers entrust to them and pool the cash to buy a mix of stocks, bonds, and other instruments that they hold in their portfolios. The mutual funds make their investments in varying proportions of securities, depending on the limits imposed by the prospectuses that they issue to investors prior to purchase.

The prospectus is essentially the mutual fund's charter. It describes the objectives that the fund's manager is expected to seek, the limitations imposed on the fund's activities, and the fees charged to purchasers to participate in the fund. The prospectus also contains the rules governing an

---

[3]Graham, Benjamin. *The Intelligent Investor.* Fourth Revised Edition. New York: HarperCollins Publishers, Inc., p. 118.

[4]Quinn, Jane Bryant, 1991. *Making the Most of Your Money.* Berrybrook Publishing Inc. Reprinted with the permission of Simon & Shuster, Inc., p. 476.

investor's buying and selling shares, including minimum amounts for initial and subsequent purchases and redemptions.

Mutual funds offered for sale to the public are required to file their prospectuses with the federal Securities and Exchange Commission (SEC). Such filings, however, do not imply that the Commission approves the funds' objectives or their plans to meet those objectives. By accepting the prospectus for filing, the Commission places the force of law behind its terms.

Mutual funds hold a range of instruments, which fall into three broad categories: stocks, bonds, and money market. At the end of September 1998, according to the Investment Company Institute, an industry trade group, there were more than 7,250 mutual funds offered in the United States. There were 3,465 stock mutual funds, 2,264 bond funds, 519 hybrid funds, and 1,023 money market funds. Stock mutual funds accounted for 51 percent of the almost $4.9 trillion in mutual fund assets, while money market funds held 26 percent of the total, bond funds had 16 percent, and hybrid funds represented 7 percent.

Stock fund managers are principally concerned with increasing their investors' capital. They invest in securities whose prices they expect will rise over time. Although growth funds may generate some income through interest or dividends, this is a secondary consideration. Stock fund classifications include aggressive growth, growth, international, and global (the last investing both in the United States and abroad). There are also growth and income funds that combine elements of growth stocks as well as income from bonds.

Bond and income funds work by providing income through the interest from the bonds that they hold and from short-term cash positions. This includes balanced funds that attempt to preserve an investor's principal while paying a current income, as well as achieving long-term growth. Balanced funds are a mix of common stocks, preferred stocks, and bonds.

Other types of bond income funds include corporate, government, global, and high-yield (also known as junk). Municipal bond funds' income is generally tax exempt to the shareholder at the federal level and ordinarily tax exempt to state taxpayers residing in the state of issuing jurisdictions.

Money market funds invest in short-term debt instruments, such as Treasury bills, commercial paper, and certificates of deposit. The goal of money market funds is to maintain a stable net asset value while paying interest. Those funds also come in two varieties, taxable and tax exempt.

As pooled investments, mutual funds offer shareholders five immediate advantages that might not otherwise be available to them: diversification, professional management, convenience, liquidity, and low initial commitment. The recurring mantra among financial professionals, managers, and advisors is the importance of investors to diversify their holdings among various asset classes. Mutual funds, by their very nature, create diversified investment portfolios because money is placed into stocks, bonds, other types of investments, and money market funds.

The principle is that not all investments follow the same price-change patterns. While some may trend up, others may trend down. Diversification cushions the effect of such moves. Even funds limited by their prospectuses to a narrow range of investment types, for example, single-state tax-exempt debt, diversify holdings across the category.

As financial professionals, mutual fund managers work full time investing the money that their shareholders have entrusted to them. They devote their attention to developments in the markets and have access to research sources that only the most wealthy investors can afford for themselves. Mutual fund managers can identify opportunities and warning signs, taking action long before individual investors even become aware of such developments.

The number of sources where individual investors may buy mutual funds traditionally has been extensive. The range of outlets is increasing, as the federal government eases restrictions on businesses in which financial institutions may engage. Some mutual fund companies have become widely recognized, thanks in great measure to large-scale marketing campaigns as well as the increasing popularity of that form of investing.

Some mutual fund companies sell to individual investors through their own sales forces, as well as through commissioned agents working for brokerages, investment firms, insurance companies, financial advisors, asset managers, banks, thrift institutions, and accountants. Funds sold through commissioned representatives are termed "load funds," since purchasers pay a fee when they buy them. Other mutual fund companies sell directly to the public without a sales charge, or no-load funds.

Both load and no-load funds are available from the companies that operate them, as well as through some brokerage houses that offer funds from a cross-section of fund operators in a sort of mutual fund supermarket. Some mutual fund companies remit a portion of their sales to the brokerage for the services it provides investors. Brokerages often levy a small transaction fee of their own to cover costs that are not reimbursed by participating mutual fund companies.

With extraordinarily rare exceptions, mutual fund investors can withdraw cash from their accounts whenever they want. Fund managers tend to keep a portion of their portfolios in readily available cash. When they want cash, mutual fund owners simply notify their funds. The funds then repurchase the shares and, depending upon the terms of the prospectuses, send a check to the investor or, at an investor's option, transfer the cash into a money market or other interest-bearing account. Some investment companies and brokerages also offer to invest the proceeds in other mutual funds. Although the price that investors receive from the sale of their shares may be more or less than they paid, they can easily liquidate their shares into cash.

Generally, the minimum amount of money required for an initial mutual fund purchase is significantly less than most brokerages require simply for a customer to open an account. Some of the more popular funds offer first-time purchases for $100, or even less, to customers who agree to buy more shares on a regularly scheduled basis. Minimum requirements for subsequent purchases usually are lower than the initial investment.

MAKING INVESTMENT DECISIONS

Although mutual fund investing may simplify an individual investor's decision, it doesn't eliminate the process. Having undertaken their research into the mutual funds universe, investors must then decide which funds fit their investment temperaments, objectives, and time horizons. Investors should take into account the results that they expect from their mutual fund investments, as well as analyze their own circumstances and temperaments.

The young or recently married may be investing for a down payment on a home. Parents with youngsters may expect that their investments will pay for their children's education. In their middle earning years, investors often are making plans for retirement income. Retirees may seek to augment income sources such as Social Security and employer retirement benefits. Mutual funds also can fit into gift plans, either while the donor is living or following death.

Risk, of course, is an element in all forms of investment. Even cash runs the risk of losing value because of inflation. Before buying shares in mutual funds, investors should fully understand their personal risk tolerances. Such analysis is not especially demanding or time-consuming, but it is crucial. The process leads to asset allocation, that is, dividing investments into the various classes, objectives, time frames, and investment styles that will form the individual investor's portfolio.

After selecting potential funds for purchase, individual investors should first read the prospectuses that fund managers are required by law to provide. If there are points that they don't understand, usually they can telephone the fund company for answers to their questions. Admittedly, prospectuses are often difficult to read. Investors may wish to look at mutual fund reports provided by such firms as Morningstar Inc. Reports on individual funds provide a wealth of information that is often more easily understood.

Individual investors should examine a fund's objectives, methods to achieve those objectives, expenses charged to investors, and historical record of performance. It should be borne in mind that funds that in the past have achieved superior records might not match those returns in the future. Funds commonly incorporate a warning in their prospectuses to the effect that there is no assurance that they will achieve their stated objectives and that past performance is no assurance of future results.

Jane Bryant Quinn stands four-square behind the value of mutual funds as a vehicle for the individual investor to grow assets. "You can rack up a superb lifetime investment record with just two or three good stock-owning mutual funds, maybe a bond fund, and some Treasury securities or tax exempts. That's all you really need to know. Investing is easy, if you buy the simple things and buy them well."[5]

Finally, there are now almost more mutual funds than individual stocks. It might be wise for investors to consult a financial professional or to use the Internet to access websites such as Morningstar, Value Line Investment Survey, and Lipper Inc., for help in choosing a fund that meets their objectives.

BEATING THE MARKET

While every investor would like to enjoy returns better than the market as a whole generates, it is an unrealistic objective. Even the most skilled professional investors and investment managers fail to exceed market returns over extended periods of time of say 5, 10, or 20 years. Some investors, however, pursue above-market returns relentlessly, and futilely, including mutual fund investors. They buy and sell in a desperate attempt to outperform the market. Vanguard's Bogle warns such investors, "If you want the fund that you own to rank among the top 10 percent of stock funds, you should be prepared for it to rank among the bottom 10 percent."[6]

---

[5]Quinn, *Making the Most*, p. 474.

[6]Bogle, *Mutual Funds*, p. 174.

The Investment Company Institute estimates that there are roughly 3,500 equity mutual funds. As of December 31, 1998, only a handful managed to outperform the S&P 500 in the preceding five years. That index represents roughly the market value of 70 percent of the U.S. equity market and is the generally accepted benchmark against which funds investing in domestic stocks are measured. Few of the S&P 500-beating mutual funds, however, are diversified among stocks in various industry sectors.

Commenting on a cardinal principle that technical investment analysts invoke, Salomon Smith Barney's Louise Yamada states that she and her colleagues "try to identify the outperforming sectors in the market." This principle can also be applied to mutual funds, especially those concentrating on industry sectors. Yamada seeks "to invest with the outperforming sectors and avoid the underperforming sectors. When a sector underperforms the market from a relative perspective, eventually and usually the price (of a stock in the sector or sector mutual fund) will also capitulate and go down."[7]

For the five-year period ending December 31, 1998, 144 stock-holding mutual funds exceeded the annual average return of the S&P 500. Table 9-1, compares the return-beating funds with the Vanguard 500 Index Fund. The Vanguard fund is composed of the stocks in the S&P 500 and seeks to match the return of the Index. Of the outperforming funds, many were sector funds, whose holdings were concentrated in the industry groups that we favor, including financial services, health care, and technology.

MATCHING THE MARKET

Having found an advantageous way of participating in the market through mutual funds, individual investors confront the question of picking the right mutual fund or funds. If the stock market holds the greatest potential for wealth-creating returns, how does that investor identify the funds that will outperform the market? Although history may be a guide to performance, there is no guarantee that last year's market beater will repeat this year, let alone in five years or decades into the future. After all, mutual fund managers are exactly that: managers. They can't foresee the future with perfect clarity. If they could, they'd all be calling in their buy and sell

---

[7]Yamada, Louise. 1998. Telephone interview by J. Patrick Donlon. Snyder, New York. 2 December.

TABLE 9-1A

Outperforming Stock Mutual Funds

Fund	Five-Year Annual Performance
Fidelity Select Electronics	37.15
Fidelity Select Computers	36.09
Legg Mason Value Prim	32.01
Alliance Technology A	30.71
Fidelity Select Health Care	30.51
White Oak Growth	30.07
Alliance Technology B	29.81
Alliance Technology C	29.81
Janus Twenty	29.58
Flag Investors Communications A	29.20
Seligman Communications & Information A	28.83
Fidelity Select Technology	28.83
Vanguard Health Care	28.43
Rydex Nova Inv	28.17
Sequoia	28.07
Reynolds Blue Chip Growth	27.98
Seligman Communications & Information D	27.96
Vanguard Growth Index	27.79
Alliance Premier Growth A	27.75
Spectra	27.54
Alliance Premier Growth C	26.97
Alliance Premier Growth B	26.95
Alger Capital Appreciation	26.82
Accessor Growth	26.74
Wilshire Target Large Company Growth Invmt	26.74
Fidelity Select Regional Banks	26.55
Fidelity Dividend Growth	26.53
Pilgrim Bank and Thrift A	26.33
Alger Mid Cap Growth Retirement	26.31
Janus Mercury	26.30
Alger Capital Appreciation Retirement	26.23
Putnam Health Sciences	26.21
Vanguard U.S. Growth	26.16
Enterprise Growth A	25.96
United Science and Technology A	25.92
Northeast Investors Growth	25.49
Davis Financial A	25.47
Putnam Health Sciences B	25.26
Pioneer Growth A	25.23
Harbor Capital Appreciation	25.15
Smith Barney Telecomm Income	25.15
MSDW Inst Equity Growth A	25.13
Vanguard Primecap	25.10
MFS Massachusetts Investors Gr Stk A	24.98
GMO Growth III	24.91
Fidelity Select Financial Services	24.88
Capital Exchange	24.87
Invesco Health Sciences	24.87

TABLE 9-1B

Outperforming Stock Mutual Funds	
Fund	**Five-Year Annual Performance**
PIMCo StocksPlus Instl	24.86
Papp America-Abroad	24.85
ISG Large Cap Equity A	24.81
Idex Growth A	24.78
One Group Large Company Growth Fid	24.76
John Hancock Regional Bank A	24.70
Fidelity New Millennium	24.63
Dreyfus Appreciation	24.61
Fidelity Select Software and Computer	24.47
Strong Growth	24.47
Idex Growth C	24.42
T. Rowe Price Science & Technology	24.39
Analytic Enhanced Equity	24.33
Janus Growth & Income	24.31
Domini Social Equity	24.31
Torray	24.16
Fifth Third Pinnacle A	24.15
Kemper Technology A	24.15
Nationwide D	24.14
Vanguard Institutional Index	24.13
Putnam Investors A	24.12
Victory Growth	24.11
Delaware Devon Instl	24.09
AIM Blue Chip A	24.08
GMO Tobacco Free Core III	24.08
BT Institutional Equity 500 Index	24.05
MFS Massachusetts Investors Gr Stk B	24.03
Chicago Trust Growth & Income	24.01
Vanguard Index 500	23.96

orders from their yachts in the Caribbean instead of crunching numbers in their cubicles.

The better question concerning performance is whether it matters that individual investors buy funds that will outperform the market. Given that stocks' historical rate of growth exceeds those of bonds and cash, as well as inflation, many individual investors are content to enjoy returns generated by stock index funds. Some benchmarks other than the S&P 500, against which specialized portfolios are measured, include the Morgan Stanley Europe, Australasia, Far East Index, measuring international stocks; Russell 2000, which reflects performance of small capitalization stocks representative of that market segment; and the Wilshire

5000, tracking the stocks in the S&P 500 plus the following 4,500 stocks according to market capitalization.

Realizing that they are unlikely to guess right consistently in buying market-beating mutual funds, neophyte and well experienced investors alike look to mutual funds that hold all of the stocks in the S&P 500. Vanguard's Bogle, whose company introduced the first such mutual fund to the public in 1976, calls the Index "probably the most accurately constructed of all of the myriad indexes of market returns. The returns generated by this diversified index correlate closely with the returns of diversified equity mutual funds."[8]

Sheldon Jacobs, editor of *The No-Load Fund Investor,* notes, "We've been proponents of index fund investing for the long-term investor for years . . . Indexing is a convenient way to obtain average market returns, which can be difficult for active managers to achieve in some markets."[9] Index funds are passive investments. Instead of conducting extensive research into the merits of the universe of stocks and other securities available to them, index fund managers simply buy and hold all of the stocks that constitute the index. For extraordinarily large indexes, managers will select a representative sampling that replicates the index. For funds modeled on the S&P 500, that means all 500 issues. Investors buying such funds automatically become part owners of blue chip companies.

Since managers buy and hold the index stocks, fund holders are always in the market. Their returns then will closely mirror the returns of the market represented by the index. Obviously, those investors will experience both the ups and the downs of the market. Index funds may have a tax advantage over most non-index funds. Because of the very low turnover, they may distribute less capital gains than do most non-index funds.

Since the share turnover, or buying and selling rate, is significantly less than in actively managed funds, commissions and other costs generally are lower for index funds than for actively managed stock funds. These reduced costs are passed along to index fund holders in the form of expense ratios well below those of most funds. S&P 500 funds tend to be among the lowest cost mutual funds, with some firms charging as little as 0.20 percent in fees, or 20 cents for each $100 in fund value.

---

[8]Bogle, *Mutual Funds,* p. 7.

[9]Jacobs, Sheldon. 1977. *The Handbook for No-Load Fund Investors.* Irvington-on-Hudson, New York: The No-Load Fund Investor, Inc., p. 7.

DOGS, DIAMONDS, AND SPIDERS (OH, MY!)

Wall Street has taken innovative steps to provide simplified financial products designed for individual investors seeking to participate in the market but who may not have the resources to make the extensive commitments involved in owning multiple stock issues. Similar to mutual funds, these products bundle many stocks into a single issue that represents the index or basket of securities that investors might find attractive in working toward their financial goals. Unlike mutual funds, the products are structured as unit investment trusts and are not actively managed. The components in the trust remain constant throughout its life.

Some such unit investment trusts are sold directly to the public, usually through brokerage houses or similar organizations, while others are traded on exchanges, as are individual stocks. One unit trust, offered by several investment firms, seeks to replicate the 10 stocks in the Dow Jones Industrial Average (DJIA) with the highest dividend yields. The principle underlying the trust is that the stocks selected are undervalued, since their share prices in terms of dividend yield are below their peers.

Popularly termed the "Dogs of the Dow strategy," the 10 issues are assembled into the trust once a year, shares of which are then available to investors, generally at a price that represents the value of the underlying shares plus a commission. As a covenant in the instrument creating the unit investment trust, sponsors usually agree to repurchase shares at the investor's option. An investor, therefore, can redeem shares at any time during the term of the trust at a price that represents the value of the shares, usually less a redemption fee charged by the sponsor. The redemption price may be more or less than the investor originally paid.

Investors usually have the option to take dividends generated by trust shares in cash or to reinvest them into the trust. At the end of the year, the sponsor dissolves the trust by selling its 10 stocks on the market. Investors normally have the option to take their shares of the proceeds of the sales or to reinvest all or a portion in the subsequent trust. The 30 Dow stocks are re-evaluated, and a new trust formed, comprising the 10 with the highest dividend yields. Upon formation of the new trust, the shares of some Dow components may replace others that have risen in value to the point that their dividend yields do not qualify them for incorporation into the trust.

Historically, the Dogs of the Dow strategy has outperformed the total DJIA. For the 25-year period 1973–98, for example, a strategy based on the Dogs of the Dow returned an average annual return of 16.2 percent, while the Dow 30 returned 13.1 percent and the S&P 500 returned 13.0

TABLE 9-2

Dogs vs. Dow

	1992	1993	1994	1995	1996	1997	1998
Dow Jones Industrial Average	7.4%	16.9%	5.1%	36.9%	28.8%	23.8%	16.1%
Dogs of the Dow	12.1	28.5	4.2	37.7	28.6	22.2	7.8

percent. Annualized returns for the Dogs, however, both outperformed and underperformed the DJIA between 1992 and 1998, as shown in Table 9-2.

A similar strategy involves buying the 5 lowest priced stocks of the 10 highest yielding in the DJIA. The Penultimate Five stocks are considered to be more severely undervalued than the Dogs of the Dow, and to offer greater potential for price appreciation. Over the same 1973–98 period, an investment in a Penultimate Five strategy would have returned 19.1 percent annually.

In January 1998, the American Stock Exchange (Amex) introduced the Diamonds Trust Series I, which represents a fractional share of each of the 30 stocks in the DJIA. Each Diamond share is worth about 1 percent of the value of the Dow. If the Dow were at 10,000, for example, each Diamond share would be worth $100. Like mutual funds, a Diamond represents a diversified portfolio, except that it is unmanaged. Since it trades on the open market, the Diamond may be bought or sold any time that the Amex is open for business. The value of the Diamond fluctuates according to the trades affecting the values of each of the 30 stocks that comprise it.

The Amex also offers Spiders, the pronunciation of the acronym SPDR for Standard & Poor's Depositary Receipts. As the name implies, each Spider represents a unit of ownership in a long-term investment trust, which holds a portfolio of common stocks designed to track the performance and dividend yield of the S&P 500. As with Diamonds, Spiders trade as common stocks, with prices fluctuating according to the prices of the stocks in the trust. Income is distributed to shareholders from dividends paid by the shares in the trust, less an expense charge. Shares may be bought and sold when the Amex is open for trading.

The Amex introduced another financial innovation in December 1998, sector index shares. The sector fund shares are exchange-traded securities that represent ownership in a fund that holds stocks that track a particular sector index, as calculated by the Amex. The indexes on which the sector shares are based are modified-capitalization weighted and track the movements of companies that are part of the S&P 500.

There are nine sector indexes, including three that closely track the investment themes that I favor: technology, financial, and consumer staples. The last includes shares of pharmaceutical companies. These instruments provide investors—first-time investors, especially—a cost-efficient way to invest in a diversified portfolio that takes advantage of the themes highlighted in this book. I recommend the Amex indexes to provide exposure to key sectors that I believe will power the markets to new highs.

CHAPTER 10

Stocks to Own
and Model Portfolios

The Dow Jones Industrial Average (DJIA), of course, is designed to reflect the changes in the U.S. economy, with emphasis on large capitalization stocks listed on the New York Stock Exchange. In general terms, various segments of domestic company stocks and similar market measures tend to follow the patterns set by the Dow as flagship. Because Dow stocks represent specific and differing market sectors, some naturally will outperform others in any given year. In fact, depending on the economy and its cycles, some stocks outperform their peers year after year.

Investors frequently look for market leaders in favored industry sectors, basing their decisions on their expectations for a stock's performance in light of the economic outlook. Market leaders, particularly those in the DJIA, also tend to benefit as much from favorable economic and market conditions as from enlightened, talented, and committed management teams. Those managers are skilled in taking advantage of favorable developments in their industries and in their markets to advance their companies' earnings performance.

Those management teams deploy assets where they expect them to grow at an above-average pace. Managers recognize the importance of loyal shareholders and work to increase the value of their shareholder holdings. They may reward shareholders with cash or stock dividends, or both. They may add to returns by implementing stock repurchase programs, which reduce supply and serve to increase the price of the stock.

We have analyzed the 30 component stocks of the Dow Jones Industrial Average and have identified 12 that we believe will reward investors with superior returns through the first two decades of the twenty-first century, from the standpoint of both market and management leadership. While their sectors may differ, these companies have a lot in common. We used five criteria in our selection process, and each of the 12 stocks met our standards for:

- seasoned management
- experience in the global marketplace
- brand name recognition
- position at the fountainhead of their specific industries
- financial strength to weather turbulence

Of course, each company has learned from the past and has a clear vision of where it wants to be 20 years from today. All have made the adjustments, restructurings, acquisitions, or strategic alliances that will ensure their presence as major players well into the future. Figure 10-1

FIGURE 10-1

Worldwide Merger and Acquisition Wave

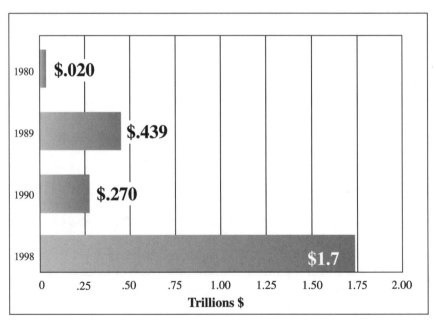

illustrates that over the past 20 years, a relative trickle of mergers and acquisitions has become a wave.

Investors seeking to develop a stock portfolio aimed at delivering returns in excess of peers in their industry, and in the DJIA, would be well served to consider this Dow dozen. Some investors might decide to pursue this sort of strategy but prefer not to make a commitment to all 12 issues. This review might constitute, therefore, a base from which investors can conduct their own analyses. They should then be in a position to construct a portfolio with fewer than 12 issues, but one that will nevertheless provide handsome returns.

AT&T CORP. (NYSE:T)

AT&T has been very busy since C. Michael Armstrong stepped into the job of chief executive officer on November 1, 1997. Since then, he has announced several major acquisitions and joint ventures while at the same time cutting costs. Armstrong's goal is to move the company away from its long distance past and into a major global telecommunications company in the digital age.

AT&T Corp.'s roots can be traced to Alexander Graham Bell's invention of the telephone in 1876. He and his financial backers formed National Bell Telephone in 1879 and controlled the telephone business, as a result of Bell's patent application having beaten rival Western Electric's by mere hours. National Bell Telephone changed its name to American Telephone & Telegraph in 1899 and became the parent of the Bell system. AT&T functioned as a regulated telephone monopoly until the 1984 antitrust settlement, which spun off seven "baby bells," or local phone companies, while leaving AT&T with long distance.

Unlike the baby bells, which did not face competition in their geographic areas, AT&T faced long distance competition from the likes of Sprint and MCI, when the FCC allowed them to link to the phone network. With the passage of the Telecommunications Act of 1996, AT&T spun off NCR and Lucent Technologies, and sold non-core holdings, such as AT&T Capital. The company was determined to focus on communication services and to reduce its dependence on long distance.

Armstrong and AT&T developed three strategies at the beginning of 1998 to grow the company. By necessity, the first was to cut costs and attempt to become the low-cost, long distance provider. The goal of this strategy is to cut selling, general, and administrative (SG&A) expenses as a percentage of sales from 29 percent in 1997 to 22 percent by the end of

1999. Assuming zero revenue growth from 1997's sales in excess of $51 billion, achieving that goal would provide more than $3.5 billion to fund new equipment and acquisitions. The company is already well on its way to meeting that goal with SG&A expenses below 25 percent on a quarterly rate basis.

AT&T's second strategy is to invest for growth. Plans call for investments in new technology, new equipment, and expanded capacity in the local, wireless, and global markets. Further investments are in Internet protocol and in AT&T Solutions, the division that is used by other large businesses to outsource their network integration and call center services.

In 1998, Armstrong addressed each of these growth strategies through acquisitions, joint ventures, and mergers. AT&T announced the acquisition of IBM's global communications network for $5 billion to grow AT&T Solutions. As part of the agreement, AT&T will become IBM's main phone service provider, and upgrade and maintain the network that carries information and provides access to the Internet.

The global market was addressed through the announcement of a joint venture with British Telecommunications to build a global Internet-based network to reach 100 cities. The purchase of IBM's global network makes that goal easier and cheaper to achieve.

In wireless, the company announced the acquisition of Vanguard Cellular systems to expand AT&T's wireless network in the Northeast, and the local market has been addressed on the consumer side and on the business side.

In the business sphere, AT&T acquired Teleport Communications Group for more than $11 billion to expand its opportunity in the local business telephone service market. Teleport, a competitive local exchange carrier, provides local phone service in 65 markets in the United States with more than 8,000 route miles in 28 states. In fact, AT&T moved so quickly in 1998 that the Teleport acquisition is the only one that had closed at the time this book was being written.

All this activity will help to ignite AT&T's growth by giving it revenue streams that are not dependent upon the ultra-competitive long distance market. Perhaps the most significant news in 1998 was AT&T's announced merger with cable giant Tele-Communications, Inc. (TCI), valued around $48 billion. The goal of the merger is to give AT&T direct access to the last mile, i.e., connecting to customers' homes and businesses, without having to pay access fees to the baby bells. Access fees have made AT&T's previous forays into the local markets unprofitable. TCI lines pass approximately one-third of all households in the United

States, giving the new AT&T the ability to compete with the baby bells in the local market.

The merger with TCI also gives AT&T the opportunity to expand its role in the Internet. The AT&T/TCI merger would not have been contemplated without an Internet Protocol (IP), the common standard that allows different computer systems, operating systems, and software to communicate electronically. IP allows all digital information, whether a television signal, telephone calls, or computer files, to be transmitted over the same line.

As Armstrong pointed out in several speeches, technology is affecting people's lives faster than ever. He observes that radio took 30 years and television 13 years to reach 50 million people. The World Wide Web reached twice that number in half the time. More than 100 million people have logged onto the Internet, and projections are for 250 million to have Internet access shortly after the turn of the century, and according to some estimates, Internet commerce could exceed $300 billion by 2002. In short, the Internet is a field in which AT&T must participate in a bigger way than at present, and TCI is the vehicle to make that happen. AT&T might form alliances with other cable companies in a move to expand its consumer reach throughout the entire country.

The third strategy that AT&T is following centers on the constant development of technology that is adaptable to many uses and transparent to customers. This will require continual upgrades of systems and programs, as well as the substantial cash that AT&T has on its balance sheet. The easy part for AT&T is announcing the acquisitions, mergers, and joint ventures. The hard part is making them work, especially with the flurry of activity in which AT&T has been involved.

Shareholders want management to own substantial stock positions and share in the risk of the enterprise, another area that Armstrong has addressed. Seventy-five percent of management bonuses are determined by company performance, versus the 25 percent in effect prior to Armstrong. Executive vice presidents are expected to own 3.5 times their annual salaries in stock, while board members are expected to own $500,000 in AT&T stock within five years of joining the board. The interests of top executives and board members are, thus, more closely aligned with shareholders.

I believe that AT&T is making the changes necessary to compete effectively in its fast changing and evolving deregulated world. Telecommunications has been growing 8 to 10 percent annually over the last few years, far faster than the economy as a whole. Although there is no way to predict the technological innovations that will have changed the world and telecommunications by the end of the first part of the twenty-

FIGURE 10-2

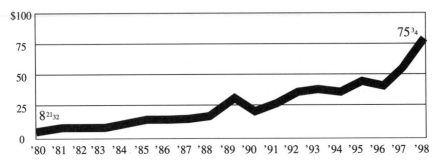

FIGURE 10-2

AT&T Corp.

first century, I believe AT&T has the right management, the right incentives, the brand name, and the financial strength to continue as a major force in its industry. Figure 10-2 illustrates AT&T's stock price performance since the end of 1980.

AMERICAN EXPRESS COMPANY (NYSE: AXP)

The almost 150-year history of the American Express Company (AmEx) is replete with examples of innovation and risk-taking, which have led to many more successes than failures. This record has formed the company's status as one of the largest providers of financial services in the world. Examples of AmEx innovation include the development of its own money order in 1868, the Travelers Cheque in 1891, and the American Express Charge Card in 1958.

American Express began its corporate life as an express delivery service in 1850, when Henry Wells and two competitors merged their companies. While associated with American Express, Wells and his vice president, William Fargo, formed Wells Fargo in 1852 in response to American Express directors' decision not to expand into California. AmEx has since evolved into a premier financial services company in charge and credit cards, asset management, and travel and tax services.

The company has three long-term goals that investors can track: annual earnings per share growth of 12 to 15 percent, return on earnings of 18 to 20 percent, and top-line revenue growth of 8 percent or better. American Express pursues these goals in part by expanding its network of card issuers and increasing the number of retailers that accept various types of American Express charge and credit cards, especially in the United States.

AmEx plans to continue to expand its international presence by forming partnerships with foreign banks that are not prohibited from issuing AmEx cards. In fact, the percentage increase in the number of cards issued is greater for international markets than in the United States. In fact, it is the company's goal to generate about half of its revenue and net income, excluding American Express Financial Advisors (AEFA), from international markets. International revenue and net income excluding AEFA represent about one-third of AmEx's revenues as of 1998.

American Express has used a segmentation strategy to differentiate its cards from its competitors' that is similar to Intel's approach, which has segmented its chips into high- and low-end markets. AmEx issues cards ranging from its high-end platinum product in the United States to a low-end blue card in overseas markets. The focus of this segmentation strategy is to retain a high percentage of customers and to increase their spending. The company introduces multiple cards into the market aimed at smaller segments while providing customers with at least one product to meet their needs.

It is much more expensive to attract new customers than to keep current customers. It also is difficult for card issuers to stand out in the flood of mass mailings offering the latest low interest rate on a credit card. It is estimated to cost between $150 and $200 for a credit card company to attract a new customer versus minimal cost to maintain a present customer.

Because AmEx imposes no credit limits, many companies issue corporate American Express cards to employees. Employers can track employee spending for budget and tax purposes. AmEx is focusing on the 40 percent of corporate card holders who do not have personal American Express cards, representing a lucrative, high-spending market. Over the past several years, the number of AmEx consumer cards issued in the United States has grown much more slowly than the number of cards issued in other countries. AmEx deliberately planned this pattern, trimming customers who were not profitable and focusing on the 35 percent of its customer base that generated 75 percent of its consumer product profit. As a result, the amount charged on AmEx cards has increased in the mid-teens on a percentage basis, far outstripping the small percentage increase in the number of cards in force.

It is estimated that credit card purchase volume overall has grown about 15 percent per year for the five years through 1998 in the United States, three times faster than the increase in overall purchases. Debit and credit cards, however, represent only 20 percent of the overall personal consumption expenditures in the country.

AmEx estimates the consumer market at $4 trillion in annual spending. *The Nilson Report,* a credit card industry publication, estimates that 33 percent of all purchases by 2000 and 43 percent by 2005 will be made with credit and debit cards.

The small business market is another key growth driver for AmEx. The company defines small businesses as those with fewer than 100 employees and sales of $10 million or less. When AmEx measured the output of American small business, it would have ranked as the third-largest economy in the world, behind only the total economies of the United States and China. The United States has about 23 million small businesses that fit AmEx's definition, which account for about half of the United States' output and most of the job growth over the past several years. The small business market is estimated at $1.8 trillion annually, with only 2 to 3 percent spent on business plastic and another 2 percent spent on consumer plastic. AmEx estimates that it has 60 percent of the small business plastic market. The small business segment is a huge growth opportunity for the company, and AmEx is seeking to become a total small business supplier through its travel, tax, and business planning services.

After a decade of losing market share in credit cards, AmEx increased its share at the expense of MasterCard in 1996, 1997, and 1998. AmEx had 20.7 percent of American credit card purchase volume in the first half of 1998, up 0.4 percent from fiscal year-end 1997. During the same period, total charge volume improved to 17.2 percent from 16.8 percent.

American Express Financial Advisors is a key element in AmEx's drive to meet its stated goals. This group fits in neatly with the overall theme of continued gains in the stock market as baby boomers save for retirement, and changes in the nation's Social Security system come under review. With more than 10,000 financial advisors, AEFA has approximately $200 billion in assets owned, managed, or administered. Revenues for the unit are derived from management and distribution fees, from the sale of mutual funds, and from the development of financial plans for clients. As the market indexes go up and more money is poured into stocks over the next decade, this American Express unit can be expected to show strong growth in revenues and net income.

American Express also is at the forefront of consolidation in the financial and travel services industries. It is the world's largest corporate travel agency, with many Fortune 500 companies under contract. The company continues to acquire smaller travel agencies around the world and bring them into the AmEx system.

Tax and business services also are an important focus, as the company acquires accounting and tax preparation firms around the country.

FIGURE 10-3

American Express Company

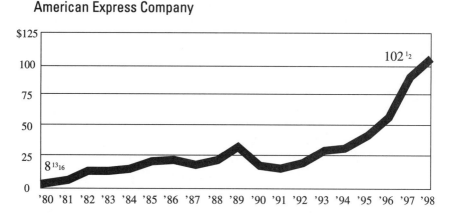

AmEx is able to cross-sell services and products to its customers, thanks to its corporate and consumer credit and charge cards, tax and business services, and financial advisory components. An investment client is a ready candidate for a credit card and for tax-planning services. A credit card holder or accounting client is likely to receive information concerning American Express Financial Advisors. The ability to effectively cross-sell products is based on AmEx's computer systems, its ability to mine data, and the strength of the company's infrastructure.

Senior management is heavily compensated based on stock price. Among senior vice presidents, 73 percent of total compensation is linked to share price appreciation; planning and policy committee members derive 86 percent of total compensation from share price appreciation, while the chief executive officer receives 87 percent of total compensation linked to the stock price. As of September 30, 1998, Warren Buffett's Berkshire Hathaway held 11 percent of AmEx shares outstanding.

Our investment team regards American Express as a core portfolio holding. The company is one of the few global brand names in financial services. It is an integral part of the increased globalization of world trade and commerce, and the desire of people around the world to save and invest. Figure 10-3 illustrates American Express's stock price performance since the end of 1980.

CITIGROUP INC. (NYSE: C)

Citigroup is a financial services powerhouse that was formed from the merger between Citicorp and the Travelers Group in late 1998. The merger seeks to take advantage of three major trends in financial services: consolidation, convergence, and globalization. Companies in the same or related segments of financial services are entering into consolidations, such as banks merging with banks and insurance companies with insurance companies. Convergence unites companies in related sectors into a single source to market a full range of products and services to consumers and corporations, among them banking, securities, and insurance.

The third trend, globalization, is a result of deregulation. Companies entering markets outside their home countries can choose to build their own infrastructure and distribution systems, which is a very time-consuming process, or to acquire financial services companies based in that market that already have the infrastructure in place. Citigroup Inc. is taking advantage of the extensive Travelers product mix and Citibank's far-flung geographic reach to strengthen each of the new company's franchises.

The company is the largest United States-based financial services firm and among the three largest in the world, based on asset size, with assets approaching $700 billion at the end of 1998. Today, Citigroup is focused on three main business units: global consumer, global corporate, and asset management. These three groups manage the products and services that have been assembled from Travelers and Citibank.

Travelers was mainly involved in the sale of insurance and in investment banking/retail brokerage, while Citibank was involved in retail and corporate banking. These four groups are approximately equal in terms of revenue. Citigroup has the size, scale, and global reach to make it a formidable competitor worldwide in all of these product areas.

The global corporate unit is composed of brokerage/investment banking, corporate banking, and commercial property and casualty insurance. The brokerage/investment banking component is essentially Salomon Smith Barney. That unit is one of the largest firms in the world in terms of retail brokerage and ranks near the top for equity underwriting, fixed-income underwriting, and municipal bond underwriting. It continues to expand globally with the mid-1998 partial acquisition of Nikko Securities in Japan.

This partial acquisition was predicated on the belief that the Japanese, who have historically had a high savings rate, will once again invest in their stock market when the country's economic difficulties are resolved. Japan also has a rapidly aging population, which usually leads to a greater proportion of saving and investment.

Citigroup's global corporate unit will operate in more than 100 countries, with more than 1,700 multinational clients. The global consumer unit encompasses all retail activities except for brokerage and asset management. This includes the branch network of the former Citibank, credit cards, life insurance, and consumer finance.

The global consumer unit is expected to be the engine for growth, as Citigroup expands its customer base and the number of countries where it does business. The Citigroup credit card operation is the largest in the world, with more than $60 billion in receivables.

Credit cards and retail branches are being used to generate leads for sales of other products and services. Citigroup's retail branches are somewhat limited in the United States, as the company has focused on international growth; nevertheless, its credit cards are used around the world. Most people who use a Citigroup credit card do not have an account with the bank, which provides a significant database to cross-sell other products, such as life insurance, mutual funds, and brokerage services.

The asset management unit includes the services offered by Citibank and Salomon Smith Barney. Combined, this unit manages more than $300 billion in assets. The largest asset management firm is Fidelity Investments, with more than $600 billion in discretionary assets. Citigroup is closing in on its goal to reach $350 billion, which would place the company close to its stated goal as ranking in the top five for assets under management.

Citigroup is seeking to increase revenue faster than either Travelers or Citibank could on its own, at the same time cutting costs. In the short term, the company is emphasizing cost control. Indeed, the company has announced $1 billion in expense reductions that will be fully implemented by 2001. That still represents less than 3 percent of total costs for the company, leaving room for potential further cost cuts. The long-term goal is to take advantage of revenue synergies through cross-selling, especially in the consumer channel.

Citigroup management has set goals that include doubling earnings every five years, which equates to 15 percent earnings per share growth annually. It has also set a goal to maintain 60 percent of revenues from recurring sources, which will help to cushion some of the volatility that comes from Salomon Smith Barney and help the company achieve a more stable and higher earnings multiple in the market.

The merger was not without risk. A number-one ranking means that competitors have a target to displace. The interests of management, employees, and shareholders, however, are aligned, because the goal is for every employee of Citigroup to own stock in the company.

Citigroup is at the forefront of the changes affecting the financial services industry. It has an unparalleled global distribution network and an unmatched array of products from insurance to brokerage to consumer

FIGURE 10-4

Citigroup Inc.

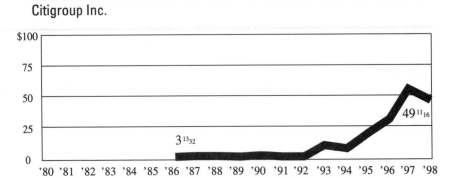

and corporate lending. The management team and employees have a stake in stock ownership and in making all of the pieces work together. Figure 10-4 illustrates Citigroup's stock price performance since the end of 1986.

COCA-COLA COMPANY (NYSE: KO)

Even as the world consumes 1 billion servings of Coke products each day, total daily beverage servings worldwide reach 47 billion. That means that Coke enjoys a little more than 2 percent of the entire market share worldwide. But since soft drinks account for only 4 percent of total beverage consumption worldwide, Coke has 50 percent of the soft drink market. The competition, however, doesn't necessarily come from the 2 percent controlled by other soft drink makers, but from the 96 percent of consumption that isn't soft drinks. Water is 42 percent of beverage consumption, coffee and tea represent 31 percent, while fruit juices are 7 percent. Coke believes that it is only starting to penetrate the 98 percent of the beverage market it doesn't have.

Coca-Cola was invented by pharmacist John Pemberton in 1886 in Atlanta, Georgia. The name Coca-Cola was suggested by Pemberton's bookkeeper after two of the original main ingredients, coca leaves and kola nuts. In its first year of sales, Coca-Cola Company sold $50 worth of drinks, while expenses were $70, leading to a loss for Pemberton.

Another druggist, Asa Candler, bought the company in 1891, and expanded Coca-Cola's reach throughout the United States and into Canada and Mexico by the turn of the century. Candler sold the company to an Atlanta banker, Ernest Woodruff, in 1919, after which Coke went public. Ernest's son, Robert Woodruff, ran Coke for the next 60 years until his retirement in the early 1980s. Under the younger Woodruff's reign, the company expanded overseas and introduced new products, such as Fanta in 1960 and Sprite in 1961.

Woodruff was succeeded in 1981 by Roberto Goizueta, who ran the company until his death in late 1997. Goizueta diversified the company with the acquisition of Columbia Pictures in 1982, and presided over the reformulated Coca-Cola in 1985. Subsequently, he refocused the company on its core products and marketing around the world. Columbia Pictures was sold for a tidy profit in 1989, and the New Coke debacle was overcome by returning to the original formula and rechristening it as Coca-Cola Classic.

In 1986, the bottling operations were spun off into Coca-Cola Enterprises, a publicly traded company in which Coke holds a 44 percent interest. Spinning off the bottling operations gave the company a competitive advantage, since bottling requires a tremendous amount of capital investment to fund new production equipment, coolers, vending machines, and related items.

The spin-off freed up the cash necessary for Coca-Cola to expand more quickly worldwide, to acquire competitors, and to increase its advertising in support of the world's best-known brand. These moves increased the sales of Coca-Cola products around the world without tying up huge amounts of capital. Combined with share repurchases and increased dividends, Coca-Cola's shareholder value greatly increased.

Douglas Ivester, who helped to arrange the spin-off of the bottling operations, is now chief executive officer. Before assuming that position, he worked in the company as chief financial officer, chief operating officer, and in assignments around the world. Ivester's goal is to double the company's volume and take a bigger piece of the beverage market.

Coca-Cola sells more than 160 brands in more than 200 countries around the world. Approximately 70 percent of the company's volume and 80 percent of its profit come from outside of the United States. Interestingly, however, about 20 percent of the world's population accounts for 80 percent of Coke's volume. Three of the top four most populous nations in the world consume less than 10 8-ounce servings of Coke products per person per year. China is at 6, India at 3, and Indonesia at 10. By way of comparison, the United States has per capita consumption of 376, Mexico at 371, and Chile at 325. China, India, and Indonesia have a combined population estimated in excess of 2.4 billion versus slightly more than 270 million in the United States. Obviously, there is an opportunity to increase sales in the future as these countries continue to grow and develop economically.

The foundation for future growth is based on a six-pack of priorities: strong brands, strong bottling system, customer focus, information technology, committed employees, and management's growth mindset. Key are the bottlers who deliver Coca-Cola products to the marketplace.

Certain bottling operations in which Coke has a non-controlling interest are designated as anchor bottlers. Anchor bottlers tend to be among the larger operations, with geographic breadth, strong management, financial capacity, and a commitment to their own profitability. These anchor bottlers distributed almost 40 percent of Coke's volume in 1997 and give Coke strong partners on every major continent. It is a system in which Coca-Cola develops and supports the brand through advertising and promotions, and the bottlers place the products in the hands of consumers. This allows Coke to localize its global strategies in individual markets. Its success is evident in Coca-Cola's having three of the top five soft drink brands based on worldwide consumption.

Coca-Cola has made its long-term goals clear to management, employees, and investors. Strategy is pointed toward these objectives: increase volume, expand share of beverage sales worldwide, maximize cash flow, improve economic profit, and create economic value added. If these objectives are reached, then worldwide volume will grow 7 to 8 percent each year on average, and earnings per share growth will be between 15 and 20 percent. These are long-term goals that the company expects to meet on average.

Obviously, with approximately 70 percent of sales and 80 percent of profits generated outside of the United States, the company is greatly affected by exchange rates. Typically, strength in one currency is offset by weakness in another. In recent years, the dollar has strengthened against almost all world currencies, and Coke will have great difficulty in reaching its targets in the short run. However, these short-run deviations give the company an opportunity to use its financial strength and bottling network to invest in countries whose currencies have weakened against the dollar. Such investments will lead to gains in market share in the long run. Further, Coke has demonstrated its long-term vision by continuing to invest in Mexico during the peso crisis in 1994 and 1995, and per capita consumption increased from 306 to 371 in just four years.

Coca-Cola is a company that I believe will continue to grow and prosper over the next decade. The company has a well-conceived and aggressive strategy that is successfully implemented by its management, employees, and bottlers. Figure 10-5 illustrates Coca-Cola's stock price performance since the end of 1980. By the end of the first decade in the

FIGURE 10-5

Coca-Cola Company

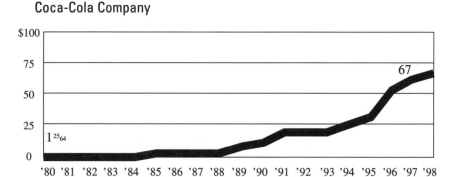

new millennium, through population growth alone, Coke estimates that the beverage market will increase from 47 billion servings a day to 54 billion servings a day. Investors can drink to that.

WALT DISNEY COMPANY (NYSE: DIS)

The Walt Disney Company is one of the best-known and most-loved brands in the world. Its animated characters, motion pictures, and theme parks reinforce each other and contribute to the Disney Experience. The company looks for future growth and brand expansion through new technology, such as the Internet; in other interactive settings, such as DisneyQuest, which offers virtual reality experiences; and in new venues, such as ESPN Sportszone, Major League Baseball, and the National Hockey League.

Disney has come a long way since brothers Walt and Roy Disney founded their animation studio. They began their film studio in Hollywood in 1923 after their first animated business failed. In 1928, Walt created the *Steamboat Willie* animated motion picture starring Mickey Mouse. It was the first cartoon to have a soundtrack. The Disney studio produced its first full-length animated feature film in 1937, *Snow White,* which was followed by *Fantasia* and *Pinocchio* in the early 1940s.

Innovation, creativity, and risk taking have obviously been hallmarks of Disney throughout the years. The company took substantial risk in opening Disneyland in 1955. No bank would finance the project, and the company tapped Walt's insurance plan to get the project started. Disneyland was a huge success from the start and led the company to acquire huge tracts of land in Central Florida for what later became Walt Disney World in 1971. The company expanded its theme park concept overseas, with the opening of Tokyo Disneyland in 1984 and Disneyland Paris in 1992.

Chief Executive Officer Michael Eisner views the history of Disney in three distinct stages. The first phase runs from the company's founding until about 1983, when the Disney name and brand were synonymous. Every toy and movie were labeled Disney. Eisner's Stage 2 encompasses the period from 1983 to 1995, when the company began to branch out and establish non-Disney labels in an effort to attract new talent to the company and to offer live-action films. Stage 3 began with the acquisition of CapCities/ABC in 1995, which was intended as a guaranteed distribution outlet for Disney products and as a launching pad for developing new channels to advance the Disney brand. Disney's entry into the Internet marketplace came with the purchase of a substantial stake in Infoseek Corp., a search and directory service that built an Internet portal business.

The Walt Disney Company has three main operating groups: creative content, broadcasting, and theme parks and resorts. The largest in terms of revenue is creative content, which encompasses Walt Disney Pictures, Touchstone Pictures, Hollywood Pictures, and Miramax, among other operating entities. This division produces and acquires live-action and animated movies for theaters and the home video and television markets, as well as developing programming for television. The creative content segment also is responsible for licensing Disney-owned characters, such as Mickey Mouse and Winnie the Pooh, and retailing through the Disney Stores located around the world.

The broadcasting division is composed of the ABC Television Network, radio and television stations, and broadcast cable. Cable properties include ESPN and such cousins as ESPN 2, as well as ownership positions in the A&E Television Network, Lifetime Television, the History Channel, and of course, the Disney Channel.

Eisner regards the synergies between Disney and ABC as a work in progress. He observes that consumers are bombarded with information and offered an expanding range of choices. Reaching them effectively requires effective distribution systems, recognizable brand names, and the strength to cut through the morass. Melding Disney's talents for creating and marketing content with ABC's distribution reach formed a global competitor in an increasingly lucrative market.

The third major Disney component is theme parks and resorts, which encompasses more than Disneyland and Disney World. It includes hotels, golf courses, Disney Cruise Line, the National Hockey League Anaheim Mighty Ducks, and baseball's Anaheim Angels. Although it is the smallest among the three main divisions in terms of revenue, it is the

FIGURE 10-6

Walt Disney Company

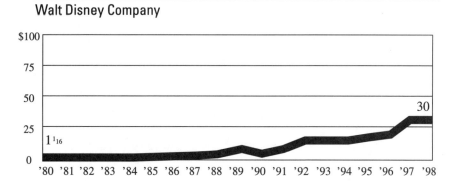

most profitable on an operating percentage basis. Further, Disney continues to expand its theme parks with construction of California Adventure. A second gate to Anaheim's Disneyland is scheduled to open in 2001, and Tokyo Disneyland also is expanding, with Tokyo DisneySea in Tokyo Bay.

Disney has a history and a brand name that are unrivaled in the media and entertainment industry. It also is a well-balanced company. If economic conditions are slow and people take fewer vacations to Disney World, they tend to increase their trips to the movies or spend more time watching television. When times are good, people increase their visits to Disney theme parks. Consequently, I recommend Disney as a long-term holding because of its strong management team and its unyielding development and expansion of the Disney brand name, as well as its diversification of assets. Figure 10-6 illustrates Walt Disney's stock price performance since 1980. In Disney's case, fairy tales do come true.

EXXON CORP. (NYSE: XON)

Much in the world has changed since John D. Rockefeller founded Standard Oil Company in 1870. Automobiles had not yet been developed and driven, planes had not yet flown, and ships were powered by the wind and by steam generated from coal. Standard Oil first focused on refining oil into kerosene and other oil derivatives, then transporting it throughout the United States, with a concentration in the eastern part of the country. Oil was first refined into kerosene that was used to light homes and businesses. Consequently, Standard Oil prospered and controlled 90 percent of the oil industry at the beginning of the twentieth century. The Standard Oil

Trust was broken up in 1911, the largest piece of which was Standard Oil Company of New Jersey, which became Exxon Corp. in 1972.

The times and technology have changed drastically over the past century, but one constant has remained: the need for oil. Exxon is engaged in all aspects of the worldwide oil and natural gas business, including exploration, production, manufacturing, distribution, and marketing. Exxon also is a leading producer of petrochemicals and has positions in coal, minerals, and electric power generation. The company operates in more than 100 countries on six continents, drilling for oil and natural gas in the Gulf of Mexico, the West Coast of Africa, and in Australia and Azerbaijan, among other sites.

The company is organized into three main groups: upstream, also known as exploration and production; downstream, the refining and marketing of final products; and chemicals. Upstream earnings represent the majority of the company's earnings, followed by downstream earnings and then by chemicals.

These three main groups tend to buffer each other. When the price of oil is high, upstream earnings are strong, while earnings for the chemical group, which relies on oil as its main input, tend to suffer. When oil prices are low, the chemicals group helps to pick up the slack. It is precisely this geographic and product diversity that reduces the company's sensitivity to volatile conditions within individual business segments and gives Exxon the strength to prosper in almost any environment.

Since the start of the 1990s, the price of a barrel of oil has dropped by more than half. This is partly a result of better exploration technology, which has extended the life of existing oil and gas fields and found new sources more cheaply. Also affecting crude oil prices are improved motor vehicle fuel efficiency and the late 1990s economic slowdown in Asia. Despite these factors, Exxon reported record profits in 1997 of more than $8 billion, the highest among public companies in the world that year.

The company maintains impressive control over its costs. Total operating costs have been essentially flat since 1990 in spite of increasing investments in plant and equipment, growing volumes, and wage increases. Profit generated per employee, a measure of productivity, has tripled over the last 15 years. The decline in the price of oil in the 1990s is changing the competitive landscape. British Petroleum's acquisition of Amoco in 1999, another original Standard Oil company, and the earlier merger between Royal Dutch and Shell Oil are driven by the belief that bigger is better in a deflationary environment for oil. This mantra continued to exemplify the merger between Exxon and Mobil announced on December 1, 1998. The combination of the two largest integrated oil companies in the United States catapults the combined company to number-one in the world in terms of annual revenue, ahead of Royal Dutch/Shell Group. This merger also recombines the two largest pieces of the former Standard Oil Trust.

The new company, if approved by United States and European regulators, will be called Exxon Mobil, with headquarters in Irving, Texas, Exxon's home. Exxon shareholders will hold 70 percent of the combined entity while current Mobil shareholders will get 30 percent. The merger between Mobil and Exxon is expected to save the combined company more than $2.8 billion per year when fully implemented in 2001. That is a significant saving, inasmuch as the combined companies would have had earnings of $11.8 billion in 1997.

The merger also will improve the combined return on capital employed to a higher level than either could have reached on its own over the same period. Increasing returns on investments, while reducing the amount of capital expenditures to produce that profit, is a sure recipe for a rising stock price over time. The Exxon and Mobil combination will also make the new company the second largest investor-owned natural gas company in the world. Only Russia's Gazprom will have larger reserves than Exxon Mobil Corp.

Consumption of natural gas is accelerating faster than demand for oil and coal, which have more pollution problems than does gas. Growth in the demand for gas is projected to remain higher than other fuels until at least 2010, according to estimates of the International Energy Agency. Natural gas-fired power plants are expected to provide up to 40 percent of the electricity produced in Europe by 2015 versus only 7.5 percent in 1992, according to a study by Anderson Consulting.

Irrespective of merger approval, I recommend Exxon to the long-term investor. As a stand-alone company, it is by far the largest integrated oil company in the United States, one-and-a-half times the size of Mobil in terms of revenue, and one of the most profitable companies in the world. Exxon invests more than $500 million in research and development annually, to improve its processes, and exploration for oil to replace and increase its reserves. Company management maintains stringent cost control and a focus on increasing shareholder value. Figure 10-7 illustrates Exxon's stock price performance since 1980.

FIGURE 10-7

Exxon Corp.

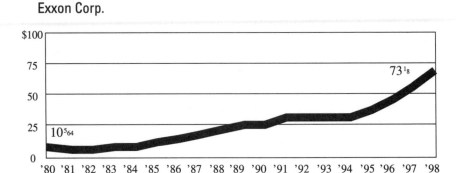

GENERAL ELECTRIC COMPANY (NYSE: GE)

General Electric is no longer merely a manufacturer of such durable goods as aircraft engines, refrigerators, and locomotives. GE has evolved into a services company that also makes excellent products. Jack Welch, GE's chief executive officer since 1981, expects that more than two-thirds of revenues will come from financial, information, and product services.

General Electric Company was established in 1892 as the result of the merger between Edison General Electric and Thomson-Houston. Thomas A. Edison was one of the company's first directors until he left in 1894. GE's focus on research and its strong balance sheet helped the company to grow in lightbulbs, trolleys, and home appliances, among other industry sectors.

Under Jack Welch, the company began to change its focus from products to services. Welch's goal was to make GE number-one or number-two in every industry in which it competes. He sold operations that did not fit that target, using the proceeds to reinvest in segments that either were or could be number-one or number-two in their industries. Under Welch's direction, GE adopted the Six Sigma program and has applied it throughout the company.

Six Sigma, a quality-control program originally developed by Motorola to reduce defects, improves manufacturing processes and reduces costs. GE has taken the process a step further and is using it to improve customer service. The goal of Six Sigma is to have 99.9997 percent perfection in all of GE's manufacturing and service processes by 2000. Achieving this goal would significantly reduce costs and the amount of capital employed, and improve customer satisfaction. As examples, achieving Four Sigma, or 99 percent perfection, would result in more than 200,000 erroneous drug prescriptions each year, two long or short landings at major airports each day, or 5,000 incorrect surgical procedures each week.

Problems in processes are the result of variability in the process. Therefore, processes are defined, measured, analyzed, improved, and controlled. The key to defining the problem is not what GE thinks the problem to be, but rather in understanding the customer's critical-to-quality factors.

GE instituted the program throughout the company by training and developing leaders to teach the process and way of thinking to all levels of the organization. Master Black Belts function as the trainers and mentors and receive more than 150 hours of training. Black Belts and Green Belts receive more than 100 hours of training.

This training, an investment in GE's future, has paid a handsome dividend. When the program was instituted in 1996, the cost of implementation was more than the benefits generated that year. The company, however, expected to save approximately $700 million over and above the costs to rework processes in 1998. That number is projected to grow every year. The total return from Six Sigma in terms of savings, improved profit margins, and other benefits has been estimated at $8 to $12 billion through 2008.

The Six Sigma program is only one of three core initiatives that the company has undertaken. The other two are globalization and product services. Continued globalization is necessary to achieve double-digit revenue growth. From 1987 to 1997, GE revenues grew 6 percent in the United States and 17 percent in the rest of the world. As of 1998, the company generated about 45 percent of its revenue outside the United States. Faster growth in Eastern Europe and China is projected to drive overseas revenue to more than half of the total.

GE's financial strength also allows it to take advantage of weaknesses in other parts of the world, to buy companies located outside of the United States and to expand its market share. GE planned to invest in Asia during economic weakness in the Far East, much as it did on weakness in Mexico and Europe in the past.

The focus on services has also changed GE over the last decade. In 1990, the sale of such products as jet engines, CT scanners, turbines, and similar items was more than half of GE's total sales. Revenues from GE Capital and NBC, among others, were about 45 percent of sales. As of 1998, services accounted for about two-thirds of revenue, with the expectation that service revenue may account for three-quarters of revenues in the future.

GE operates in eight business categories: aircraft engines, appliances, broadcasting, industrial products and services, materials, power generation, technical products and services, and financial services. General Electric Capital Services (GECS) operates 27 companies in

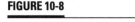

FIGURE 10-8

General Electric Company

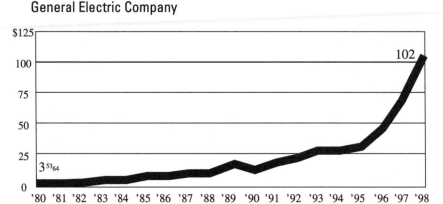

equipment management, specialty insurance, consumer service, special-ized financing, and mid-market financing. GECS represented close to 40 percent of GE's total revenue of approximately $100 billion and profit of approximately $9 billion in 1998. In addition, GECS has more than $250 billion in assets, making it one of the five largest financial institutions in the United States. It is a financial giant that has achieved rapid growth and profitability at a time when many others in the industry were not growing either their top or their bottom lines.

General Electric should be a core holding for long-term investors. Jack Welch will retire in 2000, but it is a credit to his leadership that the company has developed a way of thinking and approaching business de-cisions that goes beyond one executive. GE's strength lies in its diversifi-cation of products and services, in its worldwide sales, and in its commitment to quality, all of which result in increased sales and profits year after year. Figure 10-8 illustrates General Electric's stock price per-formance since 1980.

INTERNATIONAL BUSINESS MACHINES CORP. (NYSE: IBM)

IBM has gone back to the future to develop its strategy for growth by fo-cusing on the customer. At its founding, the company concentrated on the customer and made a commitment to providing solutions to specific cus-tomer problems.

The company's origins date to 1890, when the United States Census Bureau needed a new way to count the population in a country that was in the midst of an immigration boom. That new way was devised by Herman Hollerith, a Census Bureau employee and recent immigrant, who developed the punch card tabulating machine. The machine used an electric current essentially to scan holes in punch cards and keep a running total of the data.

Hollerith later formed the Tabulating Machine Co. in 1896. In 1911, his company merged with two other companies to become the Computing-Tabulating-Recording Co. In 1914, Thomas J. Watson, Sr., joined the company and became president within a year. Watson, famous for his slogan "THINK," focused the company on providing large-scale, custom-built tabulating machines for businesses. This concentration on creating solutions for customer problems took the company around the world, rapidly expanding sales. The company's name was changed to International Business Machines Corp., or IBM, in 1924 to reflect this global growth.

Watson Sr. led the company as chief executive officer until 1956 when his son took over and guided the company's growth from tabulating machines into computers. Watson Jr. led the company into mainframes and innovations such as the System 360, the first mainframe computer that allowed users to run the same software and upgrade specific parts of a system, as opposed to having to purchase an entirely new mainframe. Watson Jr. also developed a new way to sell technology by unbundling the hardware, software, and services, and selling them individually, as desired by the customer.

The world began to move away from mainframes when IBM started to mass market personal computers in 1981. IBM's first machine was assembled from components supplied by other companies, including a processor chip from a company named Intel. The disk operating system was made by a small company named Microsoft.

Despite introducing the first mass-market personal computer, IBM continued to focus on mainframes. It is an understatement to say that IBM was slow to grasp the changes that personal computers would bring to the world. The company continued to recommend mainframe solutions into the early 1990s when distributed computing was the present and the future.

IBM's struggles in the late 1980s and early 1990s began to change with the appointment of Louis Gerstner Jr. in 1993 as chief executive officer, the first in company history to come from the outside. Since Gerstner's appointment as CEO, he has cut costs and managed capital wisely. Most important, he has focused the company again on its customers and in providing integrated solutions to them.

IBM's revenues can be segregated into hardware sales, services, software, maintenance, and rentals and financing. Hardware sales continue to represent slightly under half of total sales but have been declining as a percent of the total, because services have been growing even faster. Hardware, however, remains important, because it is the large-scale servers that IBM and others manufacture that drive the World Wide Web.

Management, and specifically Louis Gerstner, has been responsible for the company's turnaround and rededication to its heritage.

Gerstner has signed on to continue as CEO until at least 2002. The technical ability at IBM remains second to none, exemplified in 1997 as the fifth straight year that IBM led the world in U.S. patents. Equally important, more than one-third of the company's 1997 patents are in use in its products and processes.

Integrated customer solutions are essential in a time when the Internet and network computers play such a dominant role in business and in everyday living. IBM coined the term "e-business," which describes the way that individuals and institutions derive value from the Internet. In IBM's view, e-business is about commerce, not content. It is about how companies, employees, and transactions will change over time, given the introduction of new technology. A battle is brewing, however, over the ways that new technology will be implemented: between open standards of computing, which allow seamless communication between different computers, and proprietary standards of programming, which make setting communication standards difficult.

The battle is in the competition between Microsoft, which features proprietary programming, and Sun Microsystems, Inc., which has introduced the open Java programming language. Technology alone, however, does not improve the efficiency of businesses. Rather, it is the application of the technology that helps businesses to become more efficient.

Irrespective of whether the proprietary or open school prevails, IBM is well positioned for growth. I agree that IBM's focus on the service business is the key to the company's continuing success in an environment of either open or proprietary standards, or both. Through its services business, IBM can provide and implement the technologies that contribute to the efficiencies of business processes.

The consulting group of IBM Global Services and its Value Added Network services group, for example, establish intranets that customers use as part of their business strategies. Once IBM has identified the optimal approach for the intranet to improve a client's business, the customer can access IBM's hardware and software businesses for the appropriate technologies.

IBM now supports almost all technologies, not merely the proprietary, allowing the company to work with almost any platform. It is just that type of integration of hardware, software, and services that other companies are trying to emulate.

In fact, this emphasis was probably the best strategic move that Gerstner made when he joined IBM. Gerstner decided to keep the company together when many were calling for its breakup into separate units. In a move paralleling Gerstner's approach, Compaq acquired Digital Equipment to provide services, in addition to servers and personal computers.

IBM's service teams have developed more than 250 industry-specific solutions as of the end of 1997, involving utilities and energy, travel and transportation, government, and banking and finance.

IBM estimates that the information technology market will increase to more than $1.2 trillion by 2000, compared with $800 million in 1996, with network computing accounting for most of that increase. IBM has been rewarded for its focus on the service business, which is growing at a rate faster than most other segments and is driving the company's growth. Services grew in excess of 20 percent year over year in 1995, 1996, 1997, and 1998. Service represents more than $20 billion in annual revenue for IBM and between 20 and 25 percent of total company revenues.

IBM is the only company that currently has the hardware, software, services, and people to implement integrated network solutions for clients. This ability to combine different disciplines, which is difficult for any other company to replicate, is the basis on which I believe IBM will achieve continued success in the future. Figure 10-9 illustrates IBM's stock price performance since 1980.

FIGURE 10-9

International Business Machines Corp.

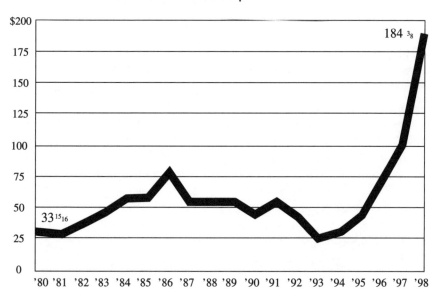

MERCK & CO., INC. (NYSE: MRK)

Merck is the largest pharmaceutical company based in the United States and is tied for first place with Glaxo Wellcome, PLC, in the world of pre-scription drugs. The company researches, develops, and manufactures human health care products and animal health products through its Merial joint venture with Rhone-Poulenc. It provides pharmaceutical benefit services through Merck-Medco Managed Care. The focus of Merck's human health care initiatives include cardiovascular drugs, inflammation and pain reduction agents, vaccines, and products for bone density, hair loss, and asthma, among others.

Merck & Co., Inc., traces its origins in the United States to 1887, when chemist Theodore Weicker arrived in the country to establish an American operation of E. Merck AG of Germany. George Merck, a grandson of the German company's founder, emigrated to the United States in 1891 and formed a partnership with Weicker. The partnership began by selling drugs and chemicals made in Germany, but started to manufacture its own compounds in 1903. One year later, Weicker sold his interest to Merck and purchased a controlling interest in the company that later became Bristol-Myers Squibb Company, a Merck competitor.

The public was first able to buy stock in Merck after World War I, when George Merck gave the U.S. government the 80 percent of the shares held by his family in Germany while he retained his own shares. Merck established its first research lab in 1933, and research has been the company's focus and major competitive strength ever since.

Research and development have sustained the company and will be critical in the future as it seeks to develop new compounds to replace several big sellers that will no longer be patented in 2000 and 2001. The company spent almost $2 billion in research and development in the 1998 fiscal year, a figure almost certain to grow as it has throughout the company's history.

The company's investment in research and development is well spent. Merck introduced nine new drugs from the start of 1995 to the end of 1997 and introduced five new compounds in 1998. These new products are expanding the number of therapeutic categories in which Merck competes. The company expects to be in 24 therapeutic categories by 2002, a strong increase from 17 in 1998 and merely 11 in 1992.

Raymond V. Gilmartin, Merck's chief executive officer, told shareholders at the 1997 annual meeting that innovation is the driving force behind Merck's growth strategy. The strategy has two parts: discovering new, breakthrough products and, just as important, demonstrating the benefits of these products and getting them into the hands of consumers.

It is this strategy that drives Merck's overriding financial goal: to remain a top-tier growth company by performing in the top quartile for earnings per share growth of leading health care companies. The company's self-assigned benchmarks include American Home Products Corporation, Bristol-Myers Squibb, Johnson & Johnson, Eli Lilly and Company, and Pfizer, Inc.

The demographics of the United States, where Merck derives the majority of its sales, certainly point to growth in the future. It is estimated that approximately 27 percent of the U.S. population was past 50 years old in 1998. By 2010, the estimate climbs to 32 percent and increases to 34 percent by 2016. Not only is the percentage of people past 50 climbing, but the U.S. population as a whole continues to increase, adding further to the effect of a bigger piece of a bigger pie. Demographics are important to such drug makers as Merck, because older people spend more on health care than any other group.

It has been suggested that the health-care industry will experience a triple effect of unit growth, consisting of population growth, multiplied by increasing consumption, multiplied by manufacturing potential. Studies demonstrate that as people age, they generally consume three times more medical products and services than in their youth.

The Federal Food and Drug Administration (FDA) has streamlined the approval process for drug applications, which means that new products can come to market twice as quickly as 10 years earlier, which benefits the pharmaceutical companies through increased manufacturing potential.

While there was concern in the 1990s that pricing pressures would drive prices down, the coming years will see higher unit growth because more people will be consuming more products. As a result, operating leverage will push profit margins upward.

Sales of prescription drugs have risen substantially in recent years, and demographic trends suggest continued long-term growth. According to IMS Health, a health-care information company that tracks drug sales, global sales of prescription drugs totaled approximately $308 billion in 1998.

Although slowing in 1998 from previous years because of economic dislocations in the Far East and Russia, worldwide drug sales increased more than 29 percent from 1993 to 1997. North America accounted for about 42 percent of global sales in 1998, up from 34 percent in 1993, as the population aged and managed care shifted more patients to drug therapies.

This increase also has been driven by consumer-oriented marketing promotions, after the FDA relaxed rules on pharmaceutical advertising in 1997. Pharmaceutical companies took note of the changes and now aggressively market to consumers, increasing their sales representatives to almost 58,000 from 41,000 in 1996.

Merck not only develops and manufactures various pharmaceuticals, it also is heavily involved in managed pharmaceutical care through its Merck-Medco group. Merck purchased pharmacy benefits manager Medco Containment Services in 1993 for $6.6 billion. In 1993, Merck-Medco managed 94 million prescriptions, and in 1998 it exceeded 300 million prescriptions. Merck-Medco covers almost one in five people in the United States, and that ratio is growing. Although managed pharmaceutical care has lower profit margins than direct sales, it does provide a conduit for drugs manufactured by Merck.

I recommend Merck for the long haul, based on its current and prospective drug pipeline, its commitment to research and development, and its dedication to managing Merck as a growth company in a future of increased opportunity. Figure 10-10 illustrates Merck's stock price performance since 1980.

FIGURE 10-10

Merck & Co., Inc.

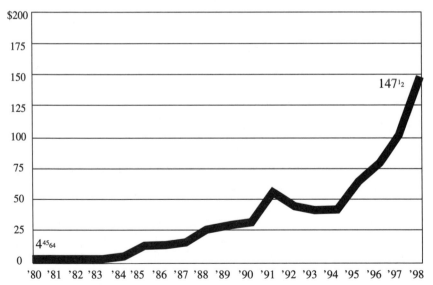

PROCTER & GAMBLE COMPANY (NYSE: PG)

Almost $40 billion in annual sales is a remarkable achievement for a company that began in 1837, making candles and soap. William Procter and James Gamble emigrated from England and Ireland, respectively, and arrived in Cincinnati on their way farther west. Procter and Gamble probably never would have met had they not married sisters, Olivia and Elizabeth Norris. It was Mr. Norris who convinced his sons-in-law to start a business together.

The rest is history and it is no small feat that Procter & Gamble Company has survived and thrived through many financial, domestic, and international crises.

Today, the company continues to innovate in terms of product development and corporate organization in order to meet the challenges of managing a global company. P&G has operations in more than 70 countries and markets products in more than 140 countries, with populations totaling approximately 5 billion.

The company's goal is to grow sales to $70 billion by 2005, approximately double its 1995 sales. When the goal was first announced, and in order to reach its objective, P&G has undertaken a sweeping reorganization. It will concentrate on sales around the world according to product line instead of organizing sales by geographic region. This move should speed the rollout of new products around the world, increasing sales at a faster rate and generating a faster return on the company's investment in new product research, development, and marketing.

The second prong of the reorganization is to centralize certain corporate functions, such as payroll, accounting, information systems, and order management. This step is expected to better serve the sales force. Durk Jager, chief executive officer, who was named the company's first-ever chief operating officer in 1995, leads the reorganization.

Procter & Gamble's strength has consistently been its brand management and product development and extensions. In the new system, the company will function under seven global business units: baby care, beauty care, fabric and home care, feminine protection, food and beverage, healthcare and new ventures, and tissue and towel.

The company manufactures and markets some of the world's best-known brand names, including Pampers diapers, Crest toothpaste, Tide laundry detergent, Ivory soap, Cover Girl cosmetics, and Crisco shortening. Approximately 75 percent of its sales are in the Western developed world, with almost 50 percent in North America and the other 25 percent in Western

Europe. P&G generates 10 percent of its sales from Asia and another 7 percent from Latin America, more than half of which is from Mexico.

It wasn't until 1993 that more than half of the company's sales came from outside of the United States. Consequently, P&G today is intensely focused on high-potential international markets, including Eastern Europe and China. The opportunity lies in increasing the number of people using company products and in increasing the number of times people use those products.

For instance, it is estimated that people in Latin America and Eastern Europe use less than half the number of bottles of shampoo that are used in North America. The use of paper towels in these regions is minute, compared to North America, and disposable diapers are less than a quarter of North American usage. Management intends to increase international sales to two-thirds of the company's total, and to generate half its profits from those sales.

Procter & Gamble employees own about 25 percent of the company's outstanding stock, and senior management compensation is tied heavily to stock price performance. Consequently, management and staff alike have incentives to reach company goals and to increase the stock price. Management also has stated its intention to increase earnings per share by 11 percent to 14 percent per year.

P&G stock has performed well over the long haul. As of December 31, 1997, the total return on P&G stock, assuming reinvested dividends, outperformed the S&P 500 for 1, 5, 10, and 15 years. The company has increased its dividend for 43 consecutive years.

The company faces stiff challenges to reach its sales and profit objectives and stellar stock performance, but P&G has the size and marketing prowess to reach around the world and a demonstrated history of reaching its goals. Figure 10-11 illustrates Procter & Gamble's stock price performance since 1980.

FIGURE 10-11

Procter & Gamble Company

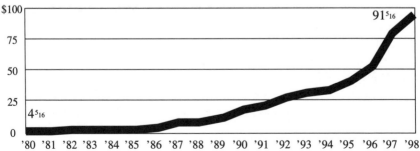

UNITED TECHNOLOGIES CORPORATION (NYSE: UTX)

United Technologies is composed of five main operating divisions, each of which is a leader throughout the world in its respective industry: Pratt & Whitney, Otis Elevator, Carrier Corp., Sikorsky Helicopter, and UT Automotive. United Technologies Corporation derives 20 percent of its sales from Europe and approximately 19 percent from Asia.

The company historically has had a significant presence in international markets, particularly aviation. The company began in 1925, when Frederick Rentschler and engine designer George Mead founded Pratt & Whitney Aircraft, the forerunner of United Technologies, to design and develop aircraft engines. Rentschler merged Pratt & Whitney with Boeing Airplane Company and Chance Vought Corp. to form United Aircraft and Transport. The new entity purchased other aviation companies, including Sikorsky, throughout the early 1930s. In 1934, United Aircraft and Transport was dissolved by the United States because of government opposition to the affiliation of airlines with aircraft equipment makers. The businesses that were spun off to form separate corporations included United Aircraft, Boeing Airplane Company, and United Airlines, all of which continue to operate.

During World War II, United Aircraft produced half of all the engines used by American warplanes. After the war, the company converted to the jet age, supplying the military and commercial airlines.

United Aircraft Corp. became United Technologies Corp. in 1975, when the company changed its name to reflect the diversity of its services and products. United then undertook a diversification acquisition campaign to lessen its dependence on government sales. This step led to the acquisition of Otis Elevator in 1976 and Carrier Corp. in 1979. The diversification has been successful, with Otis and Carrier accounting for more than 45 percent of sales.

Pratt & Whitney remains the company's largest division, with approximately 30 percent of United Technologies sales. The unit vies with General Electric Company and Rolls Royce for dominance in the large commercial aircraft engine market. Pratt also has a strong military presence, with engines designed for the F-15 and F-16 fighter planes and for the next generation of planes, including the C-17 airlifter and F-22 air superiority fighter.

Carrier Corporation, primarily known for its air conditioners, is first in the world in sales of heating, ventilating, and air conditioning units, holding almost double the market share of its nearest competitor.

Otis Elevator is the world's number-one manufacturer of elevators and other people-mover systems. Approximately half of its revenues are derived from maintenance agreements to service elevators already installed around the world. This helps to insulate the company from the vagaries of the new construction market and provides a stable revenue base.

Sikorsky Helicopter and Hamilton Standard form the Flight Systems Division of United Technologies. Sikorsky manufactures both commercial and military helicopters, including the radar-evading Comanche. Hamilton Standard provides cabin pressure systems for commercial aircraft as well as space suits for shuttle astronauts, among other applications.

UT Automotive manufactures electrical distribution systems, electronic controls, and trim packages for the automotive industry; Ford Motor Company is UT Automotive's largest customer. The division has cut costs to remain profitable in a very competitive and consolidating industry.

A recurring theme for United Technologies is its constant restructuring and attention to cost control, leading to its continued survival in any business climate. This has also been the theme of Chief Executive Officer George David, who assumed the leadership in 1994, following 18 years in various roles throughout the company.

Since taking control, David and his management team have improved profit margins each year while reducing debt and generating excess cash flow. The resulting funds have been used to repurchase shares and acquire companies in similar businesses around the globe.

In early 1999, United Technologies made two announcements that reinforced management's commitment to enhancing shareholder value. The company agreed to acquire Sundstrand Corp., which produces electrical and mechanical systems for the aerospace industry, complementing the UTX Flight Systems Division. Shortly after announcing the Sundstrand acquisition, UTX reached agreement with Lear Corp. to sell UT Automotive for $2.3 billion. Proceeds of that sale will be used to pay down some of the debt UTX incurred in the Sundstrand acquisition.

Although Sundstrand brings $1 billion less in annual revenue to UTX, based on 1998 figures, operating margins and profits actually will increase because of the Sundstand-UT Automotive swap.

The key to the improvement at United Technologies over the five years through 1998 has been its focus on its core businesses and a rationalization of capital. In short, doing more with less. That strength gives management the opportunity to expand the company and grow the business for the future in the midst of global weakness. United Technologies made acquisitions exceeding $1 billion in 1998, up from less than $300 million several years earlier. Even with the Sundstrand acquisition for $4.3 billion, the company expected to spend an additional $1 billion in 1999 and a minimum of $1 billion annually in acquisitions for several years thereafter.

FIGURE 10-12

United Technologies Corporation

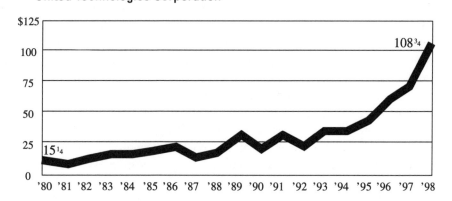

Despite the improvements the company has made, there is even more on the horizon, given its goal to improve margins in each of its respective divisions to become the best in its industry. United Technologies is a stock that allows an investor to participate in a variety of industries, including real estate and commercial and military aviation.

Older planes must be retired, engines overhauled, and new aircraft built to handle the expected increase in airline passenger traffic. Consequently, Boeing projects that more than 17,000 new planes will be needed by 2017, more than the current existing fleet of better than 12,000 planes worldwide. Further, defense budgets around the world, especially in the United States, are projected to increase after a decade of cutbacks. More buildings will be constructed around the world, as populations and incomes increase. Those buildings will need elevators and heating and cooling equipment.

United Technologies is well positioned to participate in this growth, given its investment in research and development, which exceeds $1 billion annually, and its focus on developing products and services that are profitable. Figure 10-12 illustrates United Technologies' stock price performance since 1980.

WAL-MART STORES, INC. (NYSE: WMT)

Wal-Mart is the largest retailer in the world, with a commanding presence in the United States that is just beginning to be exported to other countries. In the United States, Wal-Mart Stores, Inc., dominates its competitors as it enters new venues for growth, including continued rollout of its Supercenter format.

Sales for Wal-Mart in just one fiscal quarter are more than its closest competitor, Kmart, sells during an entire year. The U.S. retail market is estimated at $1.5 trillion in annual spending, excluding automobiles and white goods, such as refrigerators and washing machines. Despite Wal-Mart's phenomenal growth, it has less than 7 percent of the domestic market and a minuscule portion of the world market.

Wal-Mart was founded by the legendary Sam Walton, who opened his first store in Rogers, Arkansas, in 1962. At the beginning of 1999, Wal-Mart operated 1,869 Wal-Marts, 564 Supercenters, and 451 Sam's Clubs in the United States, with another 706 stores in international markets. The first store outside the United States was opened in Mexico City in 1991. The company has a strong presence in Mexico and Canada, and has inaugurated operations in South America, Germany, South Korea, and China. The Wal-Mart way—lower prices, good value, and excellent selection—sells around the world.

Growth both at home and abroad will be through Wal-Mart's Supercenters, which the company expects to grow to more than 1,400 by 2005, or an increase of 150 percent in this format. In developing markets, the Supercenters will be new construction; in other markets, the company will convert older and smaller stores to the new format. The company is also developing a supermarket format to capture more of the estimated $425 to $450 billion spent annually in the United States on food. Supplying and linking these stores is a challenge, which Wal-Mart plans to meet through extensive use of technology to manage its global operations.

A typical Wal-Mart discount store stocks more than 70,000 items, while a Supercenter has more than 90,000, many of which are time-sensitive and perishable. The company uses more than 90,000 hand-held computers in its outlets to store data and transfer them to a central database at company headquarters. That database is also linked to Wal-Mart suppliers.

The company plans to double its computing capacity to store a year of data on customer purchases. Wal-Mart's database is reported to be second in size only to the federal government's. The data can be quickly sorted to provide information by product code, store number, or purchase date, among other possibilities. The data are analyzed by Wal-Mart's buyers and suppliers, with the goal of increasing inventory of the best-selling items while reducing overall inventory.

The company also uses the data in making price reduction decisions, designed to speed the sale of slower moving items and to tailor inventory for specific geographic regions. For instance, stores in the southern

United States maintain larger supplies of fishing and hunting gear than do stores in the Northeast. The meat departments in stores in China and South Korea are stocked with live snakes, a taste that hasn't quite caught on in the United States.

Wal-Mart spends heavily on technology, with an annual budget for technology and communications exceeding $500 million. The value of that investment is demonstrated in its sales growth and inventory efficiencies. In fiscal 1998, sales increased 12 percent, but inventory increased a mere 4 percent. The company estimates that it saved approximately $1.4 billion in working capital investment. That money was used to buy back its own stock, to open new stores, and to reduce debt.

In short, Wal-Mart's use of technology gives the company a continuing and enduring advantage in the retail industry. Wal-Mart's goal is to deliver a 15 percent annual return to shareholders. That has been accomplished in the long term through double-digit increases in sales, stock buybacks, and dividends. The question concerning Wal-Mart, even as far back as 1982, has been: how long can the growth continue?

The company continues to develop new formats, to improve delivery and logistical systems, and to build new stores to generate more than its present single-digit market share of total retail spending in the United States. As of 1998, the company considered itself under-represented in the Northeast and on the West Coast. Global expansion, of course, is in its infancy.

The company also has changed the dynamics of the supply chain, with a decided shift in power from the manufacturers to the retailers. The company's margins generally increase when it lowers prices on specific goods, and suppliers have been forced to lower their prices even more. Figure 10-13 illustrates Wal-Mart's stock price performance since 1980.

FIGURE 10-13

Wal-Mart Stores, Inc.

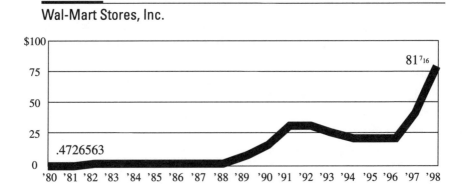

MODEL PORTFOLIOS

I have designed eight models to guide investors in structuring their own portfolios on the road to Dow 40,000. These are suggestions, not absolutes. Investors are free to follow my guidelines or to mix and match stocks from various portfolios. Of utmost importance is making selections that are appropriate for each investor's temperament and goals, and I encourage investors to consult with their personal investment advisors.

I chose only solid companies for every sector. That's why overlapping names will be noted among the different model portfolios. No matter which portfolio may be attractive, remember that investors must stay in the market for at least five years, preferably longer, in order to reap the benefits from a full market cycle. Here are a few other points to keep in mind:

- Every portfolio needs fine-tuning from time to time.
- No stock is bullet-proof.
- No matter how great a company's management or how distinguished its track record, mistakes can be made.
- Economic conditions could change the outlook for any company.

Note that in three of the model portfolios—financial, technology, and health care sectors—while it is not important to have exactly the same number of shares in each stock, the number of dollars invested in each stock should be roughly the same.

Finally, before introducing you to these model portfolios, I am required to point out that individuals in our firm, or members of their families, may have a position in and, may, from time to time, purchase or sell any of the securities mentioned.

David's Dow Dozen

This portfolio is geared toward capital appreciation with moderate risk. I term this a "Rip Van Winkle" portfolio, because it is one that an investor can buy and not look at for a year. These stocks do not require daily monitoring. The companies are so well managed that they can handle any market hiccup or short-term negative announcement.

Symbol	Name
T	AT&T Corp.
AXP	American Express Company
C	Citigroup Inc.

Symbol	Name
KO	Coca-Cola Company
XON	Exxon Corporation
GE	General Electric Company
IBM	International Business Machines Corporation
MRK	Merck & Co., Inc.
PG	Procter & Gamble Company
UTX	United Technologies Corporation
WMT	Wal-Mart Stores, Inc.
DIS	Walt Disney Company

Long-Standing American Companies with Worldwide Experience

Here is a portfolio for investors who want to have an opportunity to participate in global economic growth but do not wish to be exposed to the vagaries of international markets. My recommendation is to own these American companies that have a tradition of doing business worldwide.

Symbol	Name
T	AT&T Corp.
AXP	American Express Company
C	Citigroup Inc.
XON	Exxon Corporation
GE	General Electric Company
INTC	Intel Corporation
LU	Lucent Technologies Inc.
MRK	Merck & Co., Inc.
MER	Merrill Lynch & Co.
MSFT	Microsoft Corporation
PG	Procter & Gamble Company
UTX	United Technologies Corporation

Face of the Earth Companies

The companies in this portfolio have the management expertise and financial resources to handle just about any economic environment. They are recognizable, reliable, and profitable businesses that provide peace of mind to their investors.

Symbol	Name
T	AT&T Corp.
AXP	American Express Company
BMY	Bristol-Myers Squibb Company
C	Citigroup Inc.
KO	Coca-Cola Company
XON	Exxon Corporation
GE	General Electric Company
IBM	International Business Machines Corporation
MRK	Merck & Co., Inc.
PG	Procter & Gamble Company
DIS	Walt Disney Company
UTX	United Technologies Corporation

Fountainhead Companies in Their Industry Sectors

Trailblazers in their industries, these innovative companies are led by visionary managers. Investing in this portfolio may mean higher volatility and higher risk, but the rewards may be higher.

Symbol	Name	Sector
AOL	America Online, Inc.	Capital Goods-Technology
AIG	American International Group, Inc.	Financial
XON	Exxon Corporation	Energy
FNM	Fannie Mae	Financial
GE	General Electric Company	Capital Goods-Industrial
INTC	Intel Corporation	Capital Goods-Technology
WCOM	MCI WorldCom, Inc.	Capital Goods-Technology
MER	Merrill Lynch & Co.	Financial
MSFT	Microsoft Corporation	Capital Goods-Technology
PG	Procter & Gamble Company	Consumer Staple
SGP	Schering-Plough Corporation	Health Care
DIS	Walt Disney Company	Consumer Cyclical

Investing in the Obvious

People use the goods and services of these companies daily. That's what gives investors the confidence to stay the course even when there are challenging times in the market, or if stock prices fluctuate down.

Symbol	Household Name
AXP	American Express Company
BMY	Bristol-Myers Squibb Company
CL	Colgate-Palmolive Company
CPQ	Compaq Computer Corporation
GE	General Electric Company
G	Gillette
HD	Home Depot, Inc.
INTC	Intel Corporation
KO	Coca-Cola Company
MCD	McDonald's Corporation
PG	Procter & Gamble Company
WMT	Wal-Mart Stores, Inc.

Financial Sector

This portfolio focuses on one of the key sectors that our firm favors. Investors interested in these financial stocks must "buy the basket." It is an all-or-nothing decision. Investors should be aware that such a portfolio from time to time might either outperform or underperform the market.

Symbol	Name
AXP	American Express Company
AIG	American International Group
BAC	BankAmerica Corporation
C	Citigroup Inc.
FNM	Fannie Mae
FTU	First Union Corporation
MEL	Mellon Bank Corporation
MER	Merrill Lynch & Co.
NCC	National City Corporation
ONE	Bank One Corporation
WFC	Wells Fargo Company

Technology Sector

This portfolio represents one sector that our firm follows closely. Once again, my recommendation is to buy all of these companies to build a significant technological sector portfolio. Investors will find the greatest risk and the greatest volatility here and, potentially, the greatest return.

Symbol	Name
AOL	America Online, Inc.
CSCO	Cisco Systems, Inc.
DELL	Dell Computer Corporation
EMC	EMC Corporation
HWP	Hewlett-Packard Company
INTC	Intel Corporation
IBM	International Business Machines Corporation
LU	Lucent Technologies Inc.
MSFT	Microsoft Corporation
MOT	Motorola, Inc.
SUNW	Sun Microsystems, Inc.
TXN	Texas Instruments Incorporated

Health Care

This portfolio pays attention to the impact of the baby boom generation in the United States and to the health needs of the world's population. If investors want to participate, I recommend buying all of these stocks.

Symbol	Name
ABT	Abbott Laboratories
AHP	American Home Products Corporation
AMGN	Amgen Inc.
BAX	Baxter International Inc.
BMY	Bristol-Myers Squibb Company
GDT	Guidant Corporation
JNJ	Johnson & Johnson
LLY	Eli Lilly and Company
MDT	Medtronic, Inc.
MRK	Merck & Co., Inc.
PFE	Pfizer Inc.
SGP	Schering-Plough Corporation
WLA	Warner-Lambert Company

CONCLUSION

The Dow Jones Industrial Average (DJIA) represents about 20 percent of the $11.3 trillion U.S. equity market. It is unquestionably the most recognized symbol of American economic health. The 30 stocks in the Dow are top-quality blue chips, the cream of American industry. Historically, the

DJIA is a solid measure of market performance. The average is adjusted periodically to reflect changes in American industry. I am certain that in the future, given the dynamics of the American economy, such high-technology company names as Microsoft, Intel, and America Online are likely to be added to the index.

As a snapshot of present economic and market conditions, the Dow is probably the best measure. That is the principal reason that I have elected to concentrate on the Dow to illustrate the confidence that I have in the economic prosperity of the country and in the promising rewards that stocks offer to individual investors.

The Dow dramatically illustrates the wealth-generating power and compounding growth of stocks. A $100 investment in the Dow Jones Industrial Average of 1900 would have grown to $70 million by the end of 1998. Assuming an annual growth rate of only 9 percent, the Dow will reach the 40,000 level in 2016. A more aggressive 11 percent growth rate yields a Dow of nearly 60,000 in 2016.

I recommend that investors with a time horizon of five years and longer put their money into long-term, growth-oriented, large capitaliza-tion, blue chip companies. Such firms are led by solid management and have a history of prospering despite obstacles affecting them on literally a worldwide basis. Investors should allow these first-quality stocks to grow undisturbed, irrespective of market fluctuations.

I have identified three principal sectors in this book that I am con-vinced will lead the market higher: technology, financial services, and health care. Technology infiltrates all other sectors of the market, crossing industry lines and affecting them all. Technology is driving productivity improvements, contributing to profits.

With baby boomers at their peak earning years, the banks, insurance companies, and brokerages in the financial services sector stand to profit handsomely for the products and services they offer to this segment of the population. Baby boomers realize that Social Security will not provide the level of income they will need to fund a major portion of their retirement years.

Consolidation in the industry, exemplified by the combination of Citicorp and Travelers Insurance to form Citigroup, will create financial services supermarkets, serving a cross-section of needs through a single source. That means economy of operations and increasing earnings for those companies.

The combination of an aging population and baby boomers prepar-ing for retirement bodes well for health services, in particular the pharma-ceuticals component of the sector. An increasing number of health-care dollars will be spent on preventive medicine, and pharmaceuticals will be used as a low-cost alternative to long-term hospitalization.

Pharmaceutical companies are introducing new products in an accommodative Federal Food and Drug Administration environment. Thanks to American ingenuity and initiative, U.S. pharmaceutical companies lead the world in drug introductions and health-care innovations. As demand increases in other parts of the world, American health-care firms will become global suppliers.

In selecting the stocks that I recommend for both new and veteran investors, I have followed five criteria. The companies all feature seasoned management, experience in the global marketplace, brand-name recognition, position at the fountainhead of their specific industries, and financial strength to weather turbulence. I believe that these Dow Dozen stocks that I have highlighted in this book will reward investors with superior returns through the first two decades of the twenty-first century.

Those investors who prefer not to invest in common stocks may consider alternatives that will provide exposure to the themes that I advocate for above-market returns. Sector mutual funds, for example, also concentrate assets in specific market components, including technology, financial services, and health care. The American Stock Exchange lists indexes of various sectors that follow the same themes.

In addition, I have recommended model portfolios that take advantage of market-leading themes that investors also might consider. Note that developments in industry sectors and companies within these sectors will affect stock performance. While investors should stay the course and invest for the long term, they also should keep abreast of events, economic issues, and market activities that seem likely to affect them. The decision to buy, hold, or sell should be made in the context of historical market performance, their own tolerance for risk, and the strength of their portfolios.

The future belongs to those who prepare for it. From my perspective, the stocks of solid American companies are the future.

Welcome to Dow 40,000.

Index

Index note to reader: All graphic
representations are indicated by the numbers
in bold print.

About the Author

David Elias is president and chief investment officer of Elias Asset Management, Inc. For more than 25 years he has been advising individuals, corporate pension and profit sharing plans, and foundations. Elias is a regular guest expert on CNBC's *Today's Business, Market Wrap,* and *Taking Stock;* CNN's *Moneyline* and *Business Day;* PBS's *Nightly Business Report; CNNfn;* and has appeared on *Wall Street Week* with Louis Rukeyser, and NBC's *Today.* He has been quoted in *The Wall Street Journal, Forbes, Barron's,* and *Business Week.* Currently a contributing editor to *Chief Executive* magazine, Elias is a popular speaker at economic conferences, CEO symposiums, and seminars for investment professionals around the world. He is on the national Board of Governors of the Washington, D.C.-based Money Management Institute.